DOCUMENTS C

General Editors:

A. G. Dickens
The Director, Institute of Historical Research, University of London

Alun Davies
Professor of Modern History, University College, Swansea

THE AGE OF PEEL

edited by

Norman Gash
Professor of History, St. Salvator's College,
University of St. Andrews

Edward Arnold

© Norman Gash 1968

First published 1968 by

Edward Arnold (Publishers) Ltd

25 Hill Street, London W1X 8LL

Reprinted 1970

Reprinted 1973

Cloth edition SBN: 7131 5431 4
Paper edition SBN: 7131 5432 2

Printed in Great Britain by
Billing & Sons Limited, Guildford and London

CONTENTS

ABBREVIATIONS

Hansard	Hansard's *Parliamentary Debates*, Third Series
P.P.	Parliamentary Papers (Sessional Series)
Peel *Memoirs*	*Memoirs of Sir Robert Peel* ed. by Lord Mahon and Edward Cardwell (1856-7) 2 vols.
Peel *Speeches*	*Speeches of Sir Robert Peel* (1853) 4 vols.
Statutes	*Public General Statutes* (annual series)

INTRODUCTION

In British history the period from 1815 to 1848 was a time of distress, disorder, agitation and change. It saw fundamental political and constitutional reforms, deep sectional and sectarian controversies, much social misery and many outbreaks of popular violence. It also witnessed an extraordinary and precocious development of party politics, some epoch-making administrative innovations, and the elaboration of fiscal and financial policies which set the pattern for the rest of the century. It was in fact the formative period of Victorian Britain. Three guide-lines can be traced through this crowded scene. The first is the repudiation of the classic eighteenth-century constitution derived from the Revolution settlement of 1688-1720 and its reconstruction in terms more acceptable to contemporary society. The second is the conflict of institutions and interests – Church, Dissent, agriculture, industry, and the urban proletariat. The third is the social and administrative problem created by population expansion, urbanisation and industrialisation.

None of these issues existed in isolation. They connected, overlapped, and reacted on each other. None can be properly understood except in the context of the whole society of which they were part. Moreover, they do not in themselves tell the whole story. Though there was much talk and some reality of class warfare, at no point were social divisions absolute. Solidarity did not exist either among the aristocracy, middle classes, or working classes. Each of these convenient abstractions, though neither meaningless nor valueless, dissolves under scrutiny into a welter of subdivisions, opinions, interests, and activities. As important and influential as the more organised and identifiable expressions of special interests, such as the Chartists, the Anti-Corn Law League and the Protectionists, were the men whose opinions, sympathies and activities cut across class and economic interest. Humanitarianism, religion, political responsibility, concern for national welfare, an intellectual desire for efficiency and order, were in the long run more

effectual than class conflict or individual selfishness. The historic
institutions of the state stood up to the strain and showed themselves
capable of rejuvenescence. In an age of continental revolutions the
traditional English governing classes at no time lost, or ran serious risk
of losing, their political control. If for the young, emotional and
passionate early Victorian people their problems and grievances
blackened the horizon, the typical continental observer (which
Marx and Engels were not) saw matters differently. The social and
administrative problems of Britain seemed no worse, often less severe,
than those of European countries; its political stability and social unity
considerably greater; its industrial wealth and economic expansion
unrivalled by any other power in the world.

The changes which came with a rush after 1827 had been maturing
for over a generation. The Napoleonic Wars had paralysed the
promising reform movement of the late eighteenth century; the after-
math of war created new problems; the mere passage of time added
to the defectiveness of old institutions and to the strength of new ideas
and forces in British society. The preceding era had not been devoid of
beneficial changes in the practice and institutions of government but
they had not been of a fundamental or dramatic nature. After Waterloo
the tone of press and public comment gave evidence of a widening
gulf between government and the society to whose basic needs it
administered. Lord Liverpool's war-time cabinet found itself after 1814
facing the social and economic consequences of the greatest and costliest
war so far fought in British history. Its parliamentary support was
precarious, its administrative potentialities limited, its outlook coloured
by the misleading lessons of the French Revolution. Nevertheless it
constituted a continuing element of political stability and its disinte-
gration after 1827 led to a degree of parliamentary independence and
executive weakness that made possible the great constitutional revolution of 1828-32. The three great measures of these years – the Repeal of
the Test and Corporation Acts, Catholic Emancipation, the Reform
Act of 1832 – marked the end of the oligarchic Anglican constitution of
the eighteenth century and ushered in a period of further controversial
change.

Of the three initial measures the first (I, 4) was no more than the
formal abandonment of a principle – the statutory monopoly of public
and municipal offices by members of the Established Church – which
for a century had been little more than a legal fiction as the result of the
passing of annual Indemnity Acts, relieving Protestant Dissenters from

the actual penalties of the law. The practical protection to the Church was nil; the offensiveness to Dissenters gratuitous. As a principle the sacramental test was unacceptable to liberal minds; as a piece of legal machinery it was felt by many Anglicans to be a degradation (**I, 3**). Only prejudice, prescription and inertia had preserved these relics of seventeenth-century conflicts into the nineteenth. They succumbed almost unresistingly to the first organised attack made on them by the Dissenters after 1827 (**I, 1, 2**). Yet their repeal was also a symbol. It was the first successful attack on the legal position of the Established Church since the Revolution.

Catholic Emancipation (**I, 8**) was a different matter. It concerned the actual exclusion of Catholics from office. It raised deep historical emotions. Above all it was part of the Irish question. It was true that in educated liberal circles the notion of proscribing any class of men on grounds of religion seemed an historical barbarism; while ever since Pitt's Act of Union in 1800 emancipation was regarded by most Whigs and many Tories as the honouring of a past pledge and the only hope of an Anglo-Irish future. Against these champions of tolerance and expediency were ranged the weight of popular anti-Roman Catholicism, the Anglican Establishment and the traditional Church and King Tories. There were also the intellectual opinions of men like Peel who thought that emancipation would do nothing for Ireland's social problems, much to exacerbate its religious and political divisions, and in the end prove incompatible with the maintenance of the Union. Even the body of English Dissenters, while officially regarding the Roman Catholics as fellow-sufferers, were by no means so whole-hearted as the utterances of their leaders might suggest. Since 1806 Catholic Emancipation had been the greatest of all domestic issues; every cabinet and every parliament had been divided on it.

What ended the deadlock was the success of O'Connell, the Catholic League, and the Irish Catholic priesthood in breaking the ties of political service between the Irish county freeholder and his landlord. The election in 1828 of the ineligible O'Connell (**I, 5, 6**) merely carried one stage further the alarming demonstration of the 1826 general election. What could be done in County Clare at a by-election could be repeated in a score of Irish counties at the next appeal to the Irish electorate. Threatened by a virtual collapse of a large part of the Irish representative system, unable to rely on parliament for any policy of coercion, the government of Wellington and Peel gave way to what seemed the lesser of two evils (**I, 7**). The late and enforced concession of emancipation had this particular consequence. Had it come sooner it would almost certainly have been accompanied by 'securities' to Protestantism such as a Crown veto on Irish episcopal appointments and payment of stipends to the Roman clergy. In 1829, largely at Peel's insistence, these well-intentioned but potentially disastrous proposals were rejected and the act of Emancipation was remarkable for its simplicity. The only effort at regulation related to the religious orders and proved in fact of little significance. But however necessary and inevitable, the passage of Emancipation shook the loyalty of traditional government supporters, did irretrievable damage to Peel's reputation, and allowed parliamentary reform to emerge as the next great national issue.

When Grey succeeded Wellington as prime minister at the end of 1830, it was virtually with a mandate to pass a reform bill. What was unexpected was the nature of the measure which the ministers brought forward three months later. Grey's crucial decision was to end political agitation and strengthen the aristocratic constitution by passing a reform so sweeping that it would more than satisfy the expectations of the general public (II, 1). He miscalculated his ability to persuade the two houses of parliament of the wisdom of his policy and he was forced first to dissolve the Commons in 1831 and then to coerce the Lords in 1832. But he was right in his judgment of public opinion and from the time the country learned the details of the government's plan in March 1831, a major parliamentary reform was inevitable. Had Grey been able to anticipate the events of the next eighteen months, it is doubtful whether he would have embarked on the struggle. But once started, it was impossible for him to retreat with either safety or honour; and though his radical supporters in the country feared at times that the government's tenacity was not as strong as their own, Grey carried the bill through to the statute-book at the third attempt with only marginal concessions. Since the cabinet deliberately put forward an extreme measure because they believed that only so would it prove final, it was not surprising that the opposition should believe that the bill was more extreme than necessary, that it was the cause rather than the consequence of public agitation, and that Grey had invoked the forces of popular violence to push through a constitutional revolution which parliament alone would never have sanctioned (II, 2).

In this they had some justification; but with an unpoliced and indisciplined population, it was natural that political agitation should be accompanied by mob violence (II, 3). The lurid scenes at Nottingham and Bristol were in themselves perhaps not particularly significant though they seemed so in the context of the reform crisis. Of more importance were the political reform unions and the activities of such men as Attwood, Place and Parkes. Even this more systematic pressure from without, however, was probably more formidable in appearance than reality. It made an impressive display in May 1832 when the country came nearer to a national demonstration of civil resistance than at any other point in the history of the reform bill (**II, 5**). But the confident assertions of the extra-parliamentary radicals when talking to members of the government was not matched by their language in talking to each other. It must remain an open question whether the peculiarly middle-class weapons of organising a run on the banks and refusing to pay taxes could have been supplemented by more lethal instruments had Wellington actually formed a ministry. In any case the crisis of May 1832 was unreal. The issue was not whether a substantial reform would take place but merely whether it should be carried through by Wellington or by Grey. The good sense of the opposition politicians ensured that the duke was denied the support he needed to carry out the king's commission. As a consequence Grey won his subordinate battle with the king over peerage creations, even though the last-minute surrender of Wellington and Lyndhurst and the influence of a circular letter from the king's secretary made this ultimate sanction unnecessary. Nevertheless it remained true that the House of Lords had been coerced (**II, 4**). From a constitutional point of view this was perhaps the most revolutionary aspect of the crisis. It marked the end of a long period of equality and legislative co-authority between the two houses; it was a symbol of the ultimate supremacy of the Commons; it foreshadowed growing divergences between the political outlook of the two branches of the legislature which were strengthened by the new electoral basis of the Commons after 1832.

The Reform Act itself (**II, 6**) brought disappointment to those who had expected either that it would bring about a dramatic change in the nature of parliamentary government (**IV, 1**) or ensure the permanent victory of one political party. The Whig cabinet had certainly desired to give larger political influence to constituencies and electorates representing the new industrial, commercial and middle-class urban elements. But they had not tried to remodel the entire representative structure on uniform lines, or to equate representation with population (**II, 1a, b**). It was a selective rather than a doctrinaire reform. Moreover, an equal objective of their bill was to eliminate the grosser forms of personal and arbitrary influences working through the pocket and rotten boroughs and replace them by the more legitimate forms of influences working through classes, interests and localities. An important part of their work was the strengthening of the county representation and the direct influence of the landed and agricultural interest. The counties had been notoriously under-represented compared with the boroughs and though the inequality persisted after 1832, the balance was to some extent redressed. A consequence of the act therefore, as was realised at the time, was a sharper confrontation between the industrial and agricultural electoral interests. It was true that the social character of the House of Commons hardly altered in the generation after the Reform Act. The Anglican gentry and aristocracy possessed a parliamentary tradition which the commercial, manufacturing, and for that matter the Dissenting classes, signally lacked. The fact that M.P.s were not paid ensured that only men with independent incomes or professions, like the law, which were compatible with parliamentary attendance, could habitually look to politics as a career. What changed was not the kind of man who entered the Commons but the public, party and constituency influences exerted on him when he was there. Even so there was no sharp line between the reformed and unreformed eras. The tendency of the reformed representative system to increase the public pressures on individual M.P.s was limited by the perpetuation of aristocratic patronage, landlord influence, and the engrained electoral habits of bribery, corruption, intimidation, violence and local deference (**II**, **7**). Whether the introduction of the secret ballot, rejected by the cabinet in 1831, would have made much difference to this situation is debatable. But the agitation for the ballot in the next decade (**IV**, **6**) was an index of the dissatisfaction felt by many radicals with the practical working of the new system.

Even so, reform could not stop with the reform act. Both past tradition and current expediencies ensured the continuance of a reform programme after 1832. The first general election under the act produced a large though amorphous majority of 'reformers' (**IV**, **2**) and it was soon apparent that the most difficult and acrimonious issues would be in the sphere of religion. In the post-Waterloo era the Established Church had been the object of savage radical attacks. If its wealth and corruption were exaggerated, its structure was obsolescent and its social bias undeniable. In Ireland, as the privileged church of an alien minority, the Establishment was even more vulnerable; and Catholic Emancipation had admitted to the Commons a group of Irish Nationalists who were its unsparing critics. At the same time the repeal of the Test and Corporation Acts, while removing the major academic grievances of Dissenters, left untouched their practical minor ones: the compulsory Anglican marriage ceremony, liability to Church rates, absence of legal machinery other than parish registers for recording births and deaths, lack of burial places other than parochial churchyards, and exclusion from degrees at Oxford and Cambridge. Religious equality could not exist until satisfaction was obtained on all these points (III, 1). When in 1834 and 1835 attempts at legislative remedies broke down on the Anglican partialities of parliament, the resentment of Dissenters found outlet (III, 2) in demands for the complete disestablishment of the church.

Yet the Church, simply because it was the Establishment of the state, had its own peculiar problems. Patently in need of reform but lacking autonomous powers, it was dependent for necessary legislation on a parliament which legally had ceased to be either Anglican or Protestant. If reform was to be imposed by its enemies, the state connection which had been its guarantee might prove its undoing (III, 3). The Church in danger seemed a real cry in the mid-1830s; and though Peel's Ecclesiastical Commission of 1835 (III, 4) rescued it from its vulnerable position by setting it on the path of autonomous reform, the passions of the Church-Dissent conflict continued. The births, deaths and marriages legislation of 1836 met only half the Dissenting list of grievances and the failure of the Whig church rates bill in 1837, followed in 1838 by the abandonment of the appropriation clause from the Irish Church tithes bill, left many Dissenters bitter and frustrated. Between 1838 and 1847 the confessional conflict shifted to education because it was the one expanding field of domestic activity generally accepted as religious in character where the boundaries between Church and Dissent were not yet fixed. The Anglicans defeated the Whig scheme of 1839 (III, 5, 6) only to be beaten themselves over Graham's factory education clauses in 1843 (III, 7, 8). Revived and confident as the Establishment was at the end of the 1830s, it was unable to recover its position as a national church with prescriptive rights either to be supported by the taxpayer or to be accepted as the guardian of national education (III, 9). Paradoxically the Tractarians, who logically sought to recognise the facts of the new temporal situation and return to the old spiritual authority of the Church, in some respects weakened the influence of the Establishment (III, 8b) by the reputation for Romanism which they drew on themselves. By 1850 both sides had learned the limits of their powers and were less inclined to waste their efforts on impossible issues. Yet the conflict had not been entirely sterile. It had quickened the pace of reform and elicited new moral and intellectual energies. In improved efficiency, in the mobilisation of their own resources, and in the acceptance of greater social responsibilities, Church and Dissent showed the contemporary virtues of enterprise and competition. Though the concept of a national secular educational system (**III, 9**) had been wrecked, the early Victorian compromise of confessional effort aided by state subsidies was making a substantial and increasing contribution to educational needs as the middle decades of the century were reached.

It would be misleading, however, to regard the conflict of Church and Dissent as merely a quarrel of sects. It involved early-Victorian society as a whole and there were few national issues which it did not affect. In the central field of politics religion was probably the greatest single factor in the regrouping of parties which took place after the Reform Act. Parliamentary opposition in the 1831-2 period had been to the detail rather than to the principle of reform. Although the Conservative Party took its name from the controversies of these years, it was not clear in 1833 that Conservatism had either a party or a future. It was the attack on the Church which solidified a party of resistance, led to the break-up of Grey's ministry in 1834, and provoked the king to the dismissal of Melbourne later the same year. Peel's Hundred Days administration of 1834-5 transformed the position both of the opposition and of the chief opposition statesmen. On the one hand the situation enabled Peel to publicise his conception of moderate but safe reform and rally those elements in the electorate which had become frightened by the movement of government policy and the demands of government supporters during the first two reformed sessions. On the other, the formerly unmanageable array of 'reformers', reduced in numbers and shaken by the appearance of a Conservative government only two years after the reform act, reacted realistically by coalescing under Whig leadership. The Lichfield House Compact of 1835 was the birthplace of the Victorian Liberal Party just as the Tamworth Manifesto of 1834 (**IV, 3**) marked the emergence of modern Conservatism. It was characteristic, moreover, of this period of fundamental party regrouping that the issue on which Peel was defeated and forced to resign was an ecclesiastical one: the question of the appropriation by the state for other than religious purposes of part of the revenues of the Church of Ireland.

There were of course other matters to divide the parties. The defence of the constitution which in Conservative phraseology went hand in hand with the defence of the Church (**IV, 4**), in practice signified support for the House of Lords and opposition to further electoral reforms. The dangers here seemed real at the time even though the threats were embodied more in the language of government supporters than in the details of cabinet measures. Obstruction in the House of Lords almost paralysed at times the programme of government legislation, and between 1835 and 1837 there was a strong radical movement for a reform of the upper House. But the period of deadlock ended without an explosion. After the experiences of 1831-2 the Whig cabinet was not prepared for another constitutional conflict (**IV, 5**); and under the influence of Wellington and Peel the tory majority among the peers gradually receded from their less defensible lines of opposition. Similarly, though there was increasing pressure from the radical section of the Liberal party after 1835 for the introduction of the secret ballot in parliamentary elections (**IV, 6**), it was never adopted as ministerial policy. Some Conservatives feared (**IV, 7**) that their electoral recovery in 1835 and 1837 would drive the government to a fresh instalment of parliamentary reform. In fact the largest concession the cabinet made to its more liberal supporters was to allow the ballot in 1839 to become an open question on which the official members of the party could vote as they pleased. By that date however the emergence of Chartism and the movement for repeal of the Corn Laws, together with industrial depression and the government's budgetary inadequacies, were bringing social and financial rather than constitutional problems into the foreground of politics (**VI, 1, 2, 3**). On these the differences between the parties were not so much of principle as of tactics and competence.

Nevertheless, what happened between 1834 and 1841 was the emergence of two great political parties, rooted in the religious and constitutional issues thrown up by the events of the previous half-dozen years, stiffened by a rapid growth of central and constituency organisation to which the Reform Act itself had unwittingly contributed, and embodying definable social, economic and regional characteristics. The general election of 1841 was a landmark in the parliamentary history of Britain. It was the first time that a government with a previous majority in the Commons was replaced by a new ministry as the result of the victory of an opposition party at the polls. Only the unusual strains of the period made possible these remarkable developments in what was still by modern standards a narrow and partially corrupt electoral system. In the following decade this precarious growth was not sustained. Peel failed (**VII, 3**) to achieve an accommodation between the basic interests and views of his followers and his own conception of progressive Conservatism. Russell after 1846 failed to consolidate the forces of the left in a unified Liberal

*(but Russell defeated first
by no-confidence vote - 86-87)   - GAP, 86

Party of the kind that seemed to be emerging in the late 1830s (**IV, 9**). The party system languished in the middle decades of the century until a fresh stimulus was administered by the Reform Act of 1867. Yet substantially the foundations of the Victorian Conservative and Liberal parties were laid in the decade 1830-40.

The oligarchic nature of the governing classes and the limited electoral basis of parliament left a perceptible gap between national solutions and practical party policies. It was a gap which presented Peel and Russell with large problems of statesmanship (**IV, 8**). The more masterful man extracted his last dramatic victory at the cost of sacrificing his party position even while enhancing his public prestige. The other less able though no less imaginative man was ground down to impotence and ultimate supersession. Another symptom of the inadequacies of the political structure was the appearance between 1837 and 1848 of the two greatest extra-parliamentary movements of the century: Chartism and the Anti-Corn Law League. What distinguished Chartism from the economic Trade Union movement on the one side and spontaneous outbreaks of social discontent on the other was its demand for a complete reconstruction of the House of Commons (**V, 1, 2**). Intellectually, Chartism was both a mark of dissatisfaction with the Reform Act of 1832 and a continuation of eighteenth-century political radicalism. It was true that such a programme, aiming at mass working-class support, was peculiarly dependent on non-political factors. But to concentrate on the support which Chartism received to the exclusion of its professed objectives is to lose something of the violent contemporary atmosphere in which heroic solutions were entertained with more confidence and sometimes issued in more drastic legislation than in the decades immediately before or after. Much seemed possible in the generation of the Reform Act and much was fervently if unrealistically demanded.

It is a truism also that Chartism drew on different classes and different grievances in different regions. To explore all the social and economic causes of support for Chartism is to undertake virtually a social and economic survey of Britain. As Clapham emphasised a generation ago, only regional studies can demonstrate the complexity of the British economy at this period. Chartism, however, was not merely the sum total of regional grievances. It was the one national standard to which working men of all kinds could rally in time of distress and discontent. Yet it was almost a coincidence that the Charter, a formal embodiment of the commonplaces of radical political thought for half a century, was launched on British industrial society in time to catch the gales of the great industrial depression of 1837-42. This coincidence had two consequences. One was that the movement soon slipped from the hands of the London radical artisans and was torn by quarrels between rival demagogues and tactics (**V**, 4) which discredited its purpose and reduced its effectiveness. The other was that mass support for the movement rose and fell with the changing economic conditions of the country. Nevertheless there was a real intellectual content to Chartism: the Charter itself. It was not within the bounds of practical possibilities that an aristocratic parliament, which a few years earlier had experienced an eighteen-months struggle for the moderate provisions of the reform bill of 1831, would accept the extreme doctrinaire simplifications of the Chartist programme. But there was at all times a serious core of artisans and lower-class radicals who believed that the Charter was the only way of securing a legislature which would give them the basic conditions of life they desired. Chartism, moreover, had an effect on the governing classes which less organised and more sporadic outbreaks of social discontent might not have achieved. Increasingly it was borne home to them that some solution, whether factory acts, education, public health, church extension, cheaper living or repeal of the Corn Laws, would have to be found for what Carlyle (**V**, 5) termed the Condition of England Question.

In its different way the movement for repeal of the Corn Laws was also symptomatic of the profound tensions in British society. Certainly League propaganda made much play with arguments drawn from economic theorists. But the League only borrowed those doctrines which suited their purpose and ignored what they could also have found in the writings of the classical economists – the special connection between domestic food supplies and national security, and the undesirability of attempting sudden changes in the great economic institutions of the country. The League began as a self-confessed class affair (though the manufacturers even in Manchester were never solidly behind it) and retained something of that character to the end. Cobden was impelled by a utopian belief in the efficacy of Free Trade as an instrument of world peace; Bright by a hatred of the dominance of the landed aristocracy. It was not accidental either that the repeal movement attracted much support from Dissenters as compared with the Factory movement in which the Anglican clergy played a conspicuous role. The business men behind the League ensured a formidable financial backing, an organisational efficiency unmatched by any contemporary political party (**VI**, 5), and a use of unscrupulous methods more characteristic of cut-throat commercial competition than ordinary political jerrymandering. But there was also a passion and conviction in the Anti-Corn Law movement which was not far short of the extremism of Chartism itself. In the angry frustrated years of 1842-3 not only did the League come dangerously close to promoting Chartist disorders as a method of blackmailing the government, but in its public utterances it sought to vilify and discredit the whole apparatus of aristocratic parliamentary rule. It was not surprising that the government came to regard it as dangerous and unconstitutional (VI, 4), nor that the violence of its language provoked a counter-movement in the threatened agricultural interest (VI, 6) which made the task of securing an agreed settlement of the Corn Law question more difficult than ever.

It is clear now that both sides attached undue importance to the corn laws. Their abolition could not procure at one stroke new markets in Europe for British manufactured goods; and for another generation the prosperity of British agriculture was assured by an expanding industrial economy and more scientific farming methods. Repeal brought no dramatic advantage to the poor, though it probably helped to keep food prices down in time of bad harvests. It was true also that the whole tendency of national economic policy since 1822 had been towards a gradual dismantling of the elaborate tariff barriers bequeathed by the eighteenth century. Peel's re-introduction of the income-tax in 1842 enabled him to experiment more boldly with the tariff system; and the success of his policy between 1842 and 1845 left agriculture in a vulnerable position as the only large interest still enjoying high protection. Yet the dominant factor in the 1845-6 crisis was not the economic but the psychological importance of the Corn Laws. Their existence divided the nation, compromised the position of the aristocracy and threatened the normal functioning of parliamentary government (VII, 4). For all their massive preparations, the League could never have won a majority at the 1847 general election; but they might have captured enough seats to dislocate party rule. It was in these circumstances that the onset of the potato disease in Ireland (VII, 1, 2) exercised its decisive effect. Repeal of the corn laws could not be in a direct sense the remedy for Irish famine (VII, 3). The problem there was sheer indigence, not the inability to bring in food from elsewhere. But the famine raised a political question. Would it be possible to carry out a massive relief programme, supported by the British taxpayer and extending perhaps over more than one year, and still maintain the Corn Laws in the teeth of the League and wide-spread public opinion, and against the private convictions of many

leading politicians? Peel, and in his different way Russell, judged not.
In his closing speech on repeal and at his resignation (**VII, 5, 6**) Peel
argued that the Corn Laws must be regarded as part of the Condition
of England Question. That problem was simultaneously being attacked
from other quarters. Direct intervention by the state to regulate
general hours of work was not practicable in an insecure and savagely
competitive industrial economy and in an age when conventional
doctrine emphasised the evils of government interference with the free
play of individual forces. But even the classical economists made an
exception for women and children as unfree agents and early factory
legislation (including the important Whig act of 1833) had been concerned to defend these theoretically defenceless classes of workers.
Though the trade unions saw the advantage for male workers of
further restriction in the hours of women and children, support for the
factory reform movement from other classes in society was chiefly
inspired by humanitarian motives. The shock effect (**VIII, 1, 2**) of the
Mines Report of 1842, and the impact of Ashley's speeches in the
Commons depended almost entirely on the evidence of physical and
particularly sexual degradation involved in the employment of women
and girls underground. The powerful emotions generated by these
disclosures crowned the academic arguments of the laisser-faire
exponents. Yet they left almost on one side the question of men and
boys. It was significant that the largest alteration in Ashley's bill in its
passage through parliament was a reduction in the age at which the
employment of boys in the mines was prohibited from thirteen years to
ten. Similarly the government's factory act of 1844 (**VIII, 3**) was
primarily concerned with women and young persons; and the difference between it and Ashley's proposals was one of detail not principle.
On the main question of further reduction of hours Peel's government
preferred to mark time rather than disturb the delicate process of
economic recovery by too rapid a programme of restrictive regulation.
Three years later enough reassuring experience of the new system had
been gathered to allow parliament finally to accept the target-figure of
ten hours for which the Short Time Committees in industry (**VIII, 5**)
had been agitating. But though the controversies had centred on
women and children, the legislative benefits to the men were considerable. Indeed the act of 1847 was regarded by both friends and critics as
a major concession to the working classes as a whole. The result of all
the industrial legislation between 1833 and 1848 was that a long step
had been taken towards the establishment of a normal working day for
large-scale industry; safety precautions had been introduced for mines

and factories; and the provision of government inspectors, few in number but generally high in quality, had started a process of spontaneous development in professional knowledge and policy-making which was one of the most significant aspects of early-Victorian bureaucracy.

For all its cult of individualism, Victorian England was becoming in fact a more regulated and better governed society. The administrative difficulties of governments before 1828 in dealing with the social problems of the anarchic and discontented population which confronted them had been considerable: prejudice against state interference, the parsimony of parliament, an unwillingness to enlarge government departments, a deficiency of trained officials, and a lack of precise information. The following twenty years witnessed fundamental changes in the administration of the country. A start was made with the basic problem of law and order. London with a population of 1½ million, the largest concentration in the whole of the country, possessed only a miscellaneous and ineffective collection of parochial and ward constables, together with a number of independent police officers under separate magistrates. At a second attempt and in the face of engrained popular resistance, Peel replaced these inadequate relics of the past by the foundation (**IX, 1**) in 1829 of the Metropolitan Police. The main purpose of the new police was to prevent crime; but the question of order was also involved in the notion of a preventive police. After 1830 it was reasonably certain that at least the national legislature and government would not be exposed to direct popular violence. Peel had hoped to extend the system to the country as a whole and though he left office a year later, his force remained the model and recruiting-ground for the new local police forces slowly built in the 1840s and 1850s. The history of Chartist disorders would have been very different had all England been as well policed as London.

After 1832 the alliance between a reforming Whig government and their radical utilitarian advisers produced several epoch-making measures. The Municipal Corporations Act of 1835 (**IX, 3**), regarded by many of its supporters as merely a political corollary to the parliamentary reform of 1832, injected uniformity and efficiency into local urban government and by its provisions for street lighting and cleaning and police opened up new fields for municipal enterprise. The Poor Law Amendment Act of 1834 (**IX, 2**) set up a new public authority which through its officials and accumulated experience became a forcing-ground for administrative policy. The basic philosophy of the new poor law derived from the problem of endemic rural pauperism in

the south. It required some adjustment for the task of meeting the
periodic mass unemployment which was the feature of the industrial
districts. As it extended northward after 1837 the Poor Law encountered
widespread opposition both local and parliamentary. Not perhaps
until 1847 when the Poor Law Commission was transformed into a
Board under a parliamentary head did the new system (possibly at the
expense of some efficiency) obtain complete administrative security.
Its centralised direction and statutory powers incurred the hostility of
the anti-bureaucrats; the rigour of its principles that of the Chartists
(**V, 3**) and humanitarians. But something sharp had been needed to cut
through the jungle of the old poor law; and the doctrine of the Poor
Law Commissioners in the 1830s was harsher than their practice.
Within a decade the new administration had halved the cost of the poor
rate, done much to enforce the self-help and independence which were
to be the boast of Victorian society, and had proved that the hard-
headed as well as the warm-hearted approach to social problems had
something to offer. The effective interlocking of central and local
authorities in the poor law administration led to an increasing number
of other tasks being laid upon it, simply because no other comparable
national machinery existed. At the same time the work of the Commission led to a growing realisation that poverty was not a separate and
identifiable problem but was bound up with such other issues as
illiteracy, drunkenness, disease, sanitation and housing. The great
Report of 1842 (**IX, 4**) in its comprehensive evidence and intellectual
farsightedness was one of the greatest of Victorian social surveys. Its
author, Edwin Chadwick, had been a leading figure behind the original
Poor Law Enquiry, became secretary to the Commissioners, and was
for twenty years the authoritative if unpopular champion in govern-
mental circles of the scientific Benthamite approach to social problems.
By demonstrating the social cost of poverty, disease and high mortality,
he made the amelioration of working-class conditions a matter of
national self-interest. By his arguments for greater municipal responsibility in meeting the basic needs of urban life he weakened the laisser-
faire prejudices of his age. By his emphasis on the role of doctors,
engineers, scientists and administrators he fostered the growing
contribution which the new Victorian professional classes were making
to the science of government.

The great administrative innovations of the 1828-48 period had
the characteristics of a pioneer age. They revealed the difficulties,
formulated the lines of advance, and provided the means of action. But
they not infrequently underestimated the size of the task and the

strength of social inertia. Even in the main fields of effort much remained to be done; many other areas were left untouched. Yet by the 1851 census (**IX**, 5), the milestone marking the transition from a preponderantly rural to a preponderantly urban society, it was clear that the country had been set firmly on its new course. The unprecedented expansion of population, the steady growth of towns, the technological skills displayed to the world in the Great Exhibition of 1851, were transforming society almost under men's eyes. One inescapable mark of change was the revolution in transport created by the railroads. The building and operation of the railways (**X**, 1, 2, 3) had profound effects on the national economy in the vast outlay of capital, the creation of more employment, the increase in productivity, the cheapening of the cost of living, and the stimulation to urban development. But the social effects (**X**, 5) were perhaps as great if more intangible. Cheap travel (**X**, 4 **b**) encouraged greater mobility, broke down the provincialism of English life, facilitated administration and communication, raised new possibilities of holidays and recreation, and brought a greater sense of national cohesion. The 1851 Exhibition, itself a symbol of national unity and achievement, produced a greater and more general movement of population than ever before recorded; and it was a movement made possible only by the railways. Although it might in retrospect seem a defect that the state did not exercise more control (**X**, 4, 5) over railway construction and management, such control could only have been imposed at the cost of an enormous delay in securing a national rail network. The government lacked the money, the trained men, and the administrative experience as well as the will to enter the uncharted field of state enterprise at that date. If private enterprise was sometimes wasteful, unscrupulous and careless, no other social agency could have undertaken successfully the great railroad expansion of 1830-50. For many ordinary Victorians it must have constituted the largest single revolution in social habits that occurred during their lifetime. That such a prodigious achievement was carried out is itself a mark of the energy, optimism and resources of early-Victorian society.

I

THE END OF ANGLICAN SUPREMACY

1 A Dissenters' Protest

The General Body of Ministers of the Three Denominations was a body which had existed since 1727 to represent the Presbyterians, Congregationalists (formerly known as Independents), and Baptists in their dealings with the government of the day. The United Committee of Dissenters set up in 1827 to conduct the parliamentary campaign for the repeal of the Test and Corporation Acts had requested them to prepare fresh petitions for the 1828 session. The Rev. John Rippon was a well-known Baptist divine, pastor at Carter Lane and New Park St., London (1773-1836), and a former editor of the *Baptist Annual Register*.

At an Extraordinary General Meeting of the Protestant Dissenting Ministers of the Three Denominations, held at the Library, Redcross Street, on Tuesday, November the 13, 1827, The Rev. John Rippon, D.D. in the Chair,

It was unanimously Resolved,

1. That this Body esteem it to be a Christian duty to renew the Declaration of the injustice, impolicy, and profane tendency, of the Corporation and Test Acts; their *injustice*, in excluding Protestant Dissenters from civil and political advantages, accessible to other classes of his Majesty's subjects, not more loyal, or more zealous or active in the support of the constitution of the country than themselves; their *impolicy*, in creating divisions amongst Britons, and in depriving the King and country of the services of a large part of the people of these realms; and their *profane tendency*, inasmuch as they prostitute a supreme and holy ordinance of our religion to worldly and uncharitable purposes.

2. That they do again petition both Houses of Parliament, in the approaching Session, for the Repeal of so much of the aforesaid Acts as relates to the Sacramental Test.

Evangelical Magazine (1828), vi.21-2

2   A Call for Agitation

The Protestant Society had been established in the general renewal of Dissenting activity towards the end of the Napoleonic Wars. It was important both because of its national basis and because for the first time it united Methodists with the older dissenting bodies. It sent delegates to the United Committee and though at first doubtful of the expediency of an immediate parliamentary appeal it soon became one of the most active groups in the movement. John Wilks, an attorney and later radical M.P. for Boston, Lincs. (1830-7), was a leading dissenting layman; he had been mainly responsible for the formation of the Protestant Society in 1811.

(1827)

Near the close of the last session of parliament, the committee of 'The Protestant Society for the Protection of Religious Liberty' adopted the following resolutions, to which our metropolitan and country friends may now wisely attend.

Resolved, – 1. That THIS COMMITTEE remain firmly convinced that the honor and interest of all persons suffering under the Corporation and Test Acts required, and would have been promoted by a perseverance in the application to parliament during the present session for their repeal; but that a different opinion being entertained by some respectable public bodies in London, and by some parliamentary friends, THE COMMITTEE will rather allow a postponement to the next session than produce any schism among applicants, whose united zeal and energies may all be required. . . .

2. That this Committee cherish the hope that the numerous advocates for the repeal of these objectionable acts, of all religious denominations in the British Isles – will not allow their solicitude for success, nor their efforts for its attainment, to be relaxed by delay; – but will rather improve the interval by confirming their own purpose, never to acquiesce in a continuance of those acts, and by convincing those who are uninformed or unfriendly that their cause is just and laudable, and that they request what none but the interested, – the prejudiced – or the intolerant, would wish to deny.

3. That the Committee have been delighted by the wide spreading and noble enthusiasm with which their letters were greeted, and by the numerous and respectable petitions transmitted to other public bodies, as well as to them, and by which the House of Commons were greatly impressed: yet they would anxiously urge all congregations and other friends to the repeal of these acts, by whom those petitions were sent, to apply to their own County and Borough members to grant the measure the succor of their influence as well as their vote.

And 4. That they also intreat that all congregations who have
deferred their petitions will cause petitions to be prepared and forwarded without delay; and they assure them if they need any information, or desire to transmit their petitions through this Society, that
at the office of JOHN WILKS, esq., *Finsbury Place*, petitions will be
received and information supplied.

New Baptist Miscellany, ii.34-5 (January 1828)

3 An Anglican View

Russell moved his resolutions in favour of a repeal of the Test and Corporation
Acts on 26 February 1828 and carried a motion for going into committee
against ministerial opposition by 237 to 193. While a bill founded on Russell's
proposals received its first and second readings, Peel held conferences with the
two archbishops and other members of the episcopal bench. A form of oath
binding the taker not to injure or subvert the Established Church was agreed on
as a substitute for the sacramental test and on 18 March when the House of
Commons went into committee on the bill, Peel secured the insertion of this
declaration (4 below, para. II) to be obligatory for holders of offices in corporations and at the discretion of the Crown for holders of civil offices. The following extract from a leading Evangelical journal summarises the reactions of
liberal Anglicans both to the bill and the government's policy of conditional
acceptance.

Lord John Russell has brought forward a bill for the repeal of the
Corporation and Test Acts; the former of which requires that every
member of a corporation, and the latter all persons admitted to any
office civil or military, or receiving wages by grant from the crown, or
being servants in the royal household, shall within six months, file a
certificate of having received the holy communion according to the
rites of the Church of England, under the penalty of losing the office,
and being disabled to sue in any court, or to be an executor, guardian,
or legatee, and forfeiting five hundred pounds at the instance of any
informer. The penal effects of these acts have been long set aside by the
annual indemnity bill; but the acts themselves remained unrepealed,
vexatious though impotent, irritating the Dissenter without benefiting
the Church; and, worse than this, a parochial clergyman is legally
bound, under an exposure to heavy damages, to administer the sacred
ordinance of the Lord's Supper to the most profligate man in his parish,
who may choose to demand it at his hands, as 'a pick-lock to a place'.
Multitudes of religious persons, who differ widely as to their views on

the general question whether a test is necessary or is likely to be efficient, perfectly concur in opinion as to the gross impropriety of the particular test in question. It appears to have been at first the intention of government to oppose Lord J. Russell's motion; but the sense of the house of commons, and, as was considered, of the country at large, having been strongly expressed in favour of it, Mr Peel has consented to the repeal of the acts, upon condition that Dissenters, on taking office (those offices at least which may be thought to require it), shall declare that they will not use the power or influence derived from that office for the injury or subversion of the Established Church. In this form the bill has the support of government, and may probably pass the house of lords. We do not, however, think that the Established Church will practically secure any thing by such a vague declaration; but it will, at least, not be in a worse condition than under the indemnity act, by which neither test nor declaration was required; and it is certainly far better to have any other guarantee, if guarantee is necessary, than that worst guarantee – the profanation of the most solemn rite of our holy religion.

Christian Observer, xxviii.206–7 (March 1828)

4   The Repeal of the Test and Corporation Acts, 1828

As finally passed the bill contained two amendments inserted in the House of Lords, although by this stage it had become virtually a government measure. The first was to remove the discretionary power of the Crown (3 above) with regard to civil offices and make all of them subject to the declaration with the exception of certain categories specified in the act (clause VII). The second more important amendment was the addition to the statutory declaration of the phrase 'on the true faith of a Christian' which had the effect of excluding atheists, Jews and arguably Unitarians from the operation of the act. The amendments were reluctantly accepted by the House of Commons to avoid a prolongation of the controversy.

An Act for repealing so much of several Acts as imposes the Necessity of receiving the Sacrament of the Lord's Supper as a Qualification for certain Offices and Employments.   [9 May 1828]

WHEREAS . . . it is expedient that so much of the said several Acts of Parliament as imposes the Necessity of taking the Sacrament of the Lord's Supper according to the Rites or Usage of the Church of *England*, for the Purposes therein respectively mentioned, should be repealed; be it therefore enacted by the King's most Excellent Majesty, by and with the Advice and Consent of the Lords Spiritual and Temporal, and Commons, in this present Parliament assembled, and by the Authority of the same, That so much and such Parts of the said several Acts passed in the Thirteenth and Twenty-fifth Years of the Reign of King *Charles* the Second, and of the said Act passed in the Sixteenth Year of the Reign of King *George* the Second. . . shall, from and immediately after the passing of this Act, be and the same are hereby repealed.

II. And whereas the Protestant Episcopal Church of *England* and *Ireland*, and the Doctrine, Discipline, and Government thereof, and the Protestant Presbyterian Church of *Scotland*, and the Doctrine, Discipline, and Government thereof, are by the Laws of this Realm severally established, permanently and inviolably: And whereas it is just and fitting, that on the Repeal of such Parts of the said Acts as impose the Necessity of taking the Sacrament of the Lord's Supper according to the Rites or Usage of the Church of *England*, as a Qualification for Office, a Declaration to the following Effect should be substituted in lieu thereof; be it therefore enacted, That every Person who shall hereafter be placed, elected, or chosen in or to the Office of Mayor, Alderman, Recorder, Bailiff, Town Clerk, or Common Councilman, or in or to any Office of Magistracy, or Place, Trust or Employment relating to the Government of any City, Corporation, Borough, or Cinque Port within *England* and *Wales* or the Town of *Berwick-upon-Tweed*, shall, within One Calendar Month next before or upon his Admission into any of the aforesaid Offices or Trusts, make and subscribe the Declaration following:

'I A.B. do solemnly and sincerely, in the Presence of God, profess, testify, and declare, upon the true Faith of a Christian, That I will never exercise any Power, Authority, or Influence which I may possess by virtue of the Office of   to injure or weaken the Protestant Church as it is by Law established in *England*, or to disturb the said Church, or the Bishops and Clergy of the said Church in the Possession of any Rights or Privileges to which such Church, or the said Bishops and Clergy, are or may be by Law entitled.'

III. [The declaration to be made before the usual persons charged with administering the oaths of office or in default of such before two justices of the peace and to be officially recorded.]

V. And be it further enacted, That every Person who shall hereafter be admitted into any Office or Employment, or who shall accept from His Majesty, His Heirs and Successors, any Patent, Grant, or Commission, and who by his Admittance into such Office or Employment or Place of Trust, or by his Acceptance of such Patent, Grant or Commission, or by the Receipt of any Pay, Salary, Fee, or Wages by reason thereof, would by the Laws in force immediately before the passing of this Act have been required to take the Sacrament of the Lord's Supper according to the Rites and Usage of the Church of *England*, shall within Six Calendar Months after his Admission to such Office, Employment, or Place of Trust, or his Acceptance of such Patent, Grant. or Commission, make and subscribe the aforesaid Declaration, or in Default thereof his Appointment to such Office, Employment, or Place of Trust, and such Patent, Grant, or Commission, shall be wholly void.

VI. [The declaration to be made and registered in the Court of Chancery, King's Bench or Quarter Sessions.]

VII. [Naval officers below the rank of rear admiral, military officers below the rank of major-general in the army or colonel in the militia, and customs, excise, tax and revenue officers exempted from taking the declaration.]

Statutes (9 Geo. IV cap. 17)

5   O'Connell's Election Manifesto, 1828

To fill one of the vacancies left by the resignation of Huskisson and his followers from Wellington's government in May 1828, Vesey Fitzgerald was promoted to the Presidency of the Board of Trade. This necessitated his re-election for his constituency of Co. Clare. Since he was one of the better Irish landlords, on friendly terms with the Roman Catholic Church, and a supporter of Catholic Emancipation, there seemed little danger. It was in fact because of the difficulty of finding any candidate likely to defeat him that in the end O'Connell was persuaded to announce on 24 June that he would offer himself as candidate.

TO THE ELECTORS OF THE COUNTY OF CLARE,

Dublin, June 1828

Fellow Countrymen,

Your county wants a representative. I respectfully solicit your suffrages, to raise me to that station.

Of my qualification to fill that station, I leave you to judge. The habits of public speaking, and many, many years of public business, render me, perhaps equally suited with most men to attend to the interest of Ireland in Parliament.

You will be told I am not qualified to be elected: the assertion, my friends, is untrue. – I am qualified to be elected, and to be your representative. It is true that as a Catholic, I cannot, and of course never will, take the oaths at present prescribed to members of Parliament; but the authority which created these oaths (the Parliament), can abrogate them: and I entertain a confident hope that, if you elect me, the most bigotted of our enemies will see the necessity of removing from the chosen representative of the people, an obstacle which would prevent him from doing his duty to his King and to his country.

The oath at present required by law is, 'that the sacrifice of the mass, and the invocation of the blessed Virgin Mary, and other saints, as now practised in the church of Rome, are impious and idolatrous.' Of course, I will never stain my soul with such an oath: I leave that to my honourable opponent, Mr Vesey Fitzgerald; he has often taken that horrible oath; he is ready to take it again, and asks your votes to enable him so to swear. I would rather be torn limb from limb than take it. Electors of the county of Clare! choose between me, who abominates that oath, and Mr Vesey Fitzgerald, who has sworn it full twenty times! Return me to Parliament, and it is probable that such a blasphemous oath will be abolished for ever. As your representative, I will try the question with the friends in Parliament of Mr Vesey Fitzgerald. – They may send me to prison. – I am ready to go there to promote the cause of the Catholics, and of universal liberty. The discussion which the attempt to exclude your representative from the House of Commons must excite, will create a sensation all over Europe, and produce such a burst of contemptuous indignation against British bigotry, in every enlightened country in the world, that the voice of all the great and good in England, Scotland, and Ireland, being joined to the universal shout of the nations of the earth, will overpower every opposition and render it impossible for Peel and Wellington any longer to close the doors of the constitution against the Catholics of Ireland.

Electors of the county of Clare! Mr Vesey Fitzgerald claims as his only merit, that he is a friend to the Catholics – why, I am a Catholic myself; and if he be sincerely our friend, let him vote for me, and raise before the British empire the Catholic question in my humble person, in the way most propitious to my final success. But no, fellow countrymen, no; he will make no sacrifice to that cause, he will call himself your friend, and act the part of your worst and most unrelenting enemy. . . .

If you return me to Parliament, I pledge myself to vote for every measure favourable to radical reform in the representative system, so that the House of Commons may truly, as our Catholic ancestors intended it should do, represent all the people.

To vote for the repeal of the Vestry bill, the sub-letting act, and the Grand Jury laws.

To vote for the diminution and more equal distribution of the overgrown wealth of the established church in Ireland, so that the surplus may be restored to the sustentation of the poor, the aged, and the infirm.

To vote for every measure of retrenchment and reduction of the national expenditure, so as to relieve the people from the burdens of taxation, and to bring the question of the repeal of the Union, at the earliest possible period, before the consideration of the legislature.

Electors of the county of Clare! choose between me and Mr Vesey Fitzgerald; choose between him who has so long cultivated his own interest, and one who seeks only to advance yours; choose between the sworn libeller of the Catholic faith, and one who has devoted his early life to your cause; who has consumed his manhood in a struggle for your liberties, and who has ever lived, and is ready to die for the integrity, the honour, the purity, of the Catholic faith, and the promotion of Irish freedom and happiness.

Your faithful servant,

DANIEL O'CONNELL

R. Huish, *Memoirs of Daniel O'Connell* (1836), pp. 438-40

6   The County Clare Election

The final figures for the election were: O'Connell, 2,057; Fitzgerald, 982. The significant aspect was the widespread defection of electors from their normal political allegiance to their landlords and the demonstration by the Roman Catholic Church and the Catholic Association of their effective control of the Irish peasantry. The government were warned by a senior police officer who was sent down to observe the election that the split in Irish society was beginning to affect the police and constabulary.

Mr Vesey Fitzgerald to Mr Peel

Ennis, July 5, 1828 (at night)

MY DEAR PEEL,

The election, thank God, is over, and I do feel happy in its being terminated, notwithstanding its result.

I have polled all the gentry and all the fifty-pound freeholders – the gentry to a man.

Of others I have polled a few tenants of [*illegible*] only, my own, and not much besides what adhered to me in that way.

All the great interests broke down, and the desertion has been universal. Such a scene as we have had! Such a tremendous prospect as it opens to us!

My aim has been from the beginning to preserve good temper, and to keep down the feelings of my excited friends.

The conduct of the priests has passed all that you could picture to yourself.

The Sheriff declared the numbers to-night. To go on would have been idle. I have kept on for five days, and it was a hopeless contest from the first. Everything was against me. Indeed I do not understand how I have not been beaten by a greater majority.

The Sheriff has made a special Return, and you will say a strange one; but it will force Parliament instantly to take it up. It states that I was proposed, being a Protestant, as a fit person to represent the county in Parliament; that Mr O'Connell, a Roman Catholic, was also proposed; that he, O'Connell, had declared before the Sheriff that he was a Roman Catholic, and intended to continue a Roman Catholic.

It states that a protest was made by the electors against his return; as well as the certificate that he was called to the Bar as a Roman Catholic.

It states the numbers for each candidate – and thus it leaves the Return.

I shall see you soon, I trust. I shall be able to get away from here, I hope, on Monday. I must have a day's rest, and one day to settle my accounts, and, as far as I can, arrange respecting them.

I care not for anything since I have terminated the contest. For the degradation of the county I feel deeply, and the organization exhibited is so complete and so formidable that no man can contemplate without alarm what is to follow in this wretched country.

Ever yours affectionately,

W. V. FITZGERALD

Peel *Memoirs*, i.113-15

AOP B

7   Mr Peel's Memorandum, 12 January 1829

By January 1829 the situation confronting Wellington was that the king was still delaying a decision on cabinet discussions; the bishops consulted had almost all expressed opposition; Peel had not altered his determination to resign; the government had been obliged to dismiss the Lord Lieutenant of Ireland, Lord Anglesey, for pursuing a liberal policy of his own; parliament was due to meet early in February; and enough had already leaked out about the prime minister's views to rouse public speculation. In these circumstances Peel wrote the following memorandum to be laid before the king and sent it to Wellington with a note expressing his readiness to stay in office, if the prime minister thought his resignation an insuperable obstacle to the passage of Catholic Emancipation. On 14 January the duke delivered the memorandum to the king and after interviewing those cabinet members previously opposed to emancipation, George IV gave his permission for the matter to be formally considered by the cabinet.

I think that the Roman Catholic Question can no longer remain what is called an open question, but that some definite course must be taken with respect to it by His Majesty's servants in their collective capacity.

It is not consistent with the character of the Government – with the proper exercise of authority in Ireland – nor with the permanent interests of the Protestant Establishments – that the Roman Catholic Question should continue to be thrown loose upon the country – the King's Ministers maintaining neutrality, and expressing no opinion in common upon the subject.

Experience must have convinced us that neither a divided Government in Ireland, not a Government in that country united in opinion, but acting under a divided Government in this, can administer the law with that vigour and authority which are requisite in the present condition of Irish affairs. . . .

The more I consider the subject the more I am satisfied that a Government ought to make its choice between two courses of action, either to offer united and unqualified resistance to the grant of further privileges to the Roman Catholics, or to undertake to consider without delay the whole state of Ireland, and to attempt to make some satisfactory adjustment on the various points which are involved in what is called the Catholic Question.

If it be admitted that such are the alternatives, it remains to be considered which of the two it is most practicable or most expedient to adopt.

Can the first be adopted? Can a Government be formed on the

principle of unqualified resistance, which shall be composed of persons of sufficient ability and experience in public life to fill with credit the high offices of the State, and which can command such a majority of the House of Commons as shall enable it to maintain the principle on which it is founded, and to transact the public business?

I think it must be granted that the failure of such a Government – either through its sudden dissolution or its inability to conduct public business on account of its weakness in the House of Commons – would have a prejudicial effect generally, and particularly in reference to the Catholic Question. It would surely render some settlement of the question in the way of concession unavoidable, and would in all probability materially diminish the chances of a safe and satisfactory settlement.

No man can therefore honestly advise the formation of an exclusive Protestant Government, unless he believes that it can maintain its ground, and can conduct with credit and success the general administration of the country.

The present state of the House of Commons appears to me an insuperable obstacle, if there were no other, to the successful issue of this experiment. . . . There are other considerations which incline me to think that the attempt to settle that question should be made. . . .

First – There is the evil of continued division between two branches of the Legislature on a great constitutional question.

Secondly – The power of the Roman Catholics is unduly increased by the House of Commons repeatedly pronouncing an opinion in their favour. There are many points in regard to the Roman Catholic religion and Roman Catholic proceedings in Ireland, on which Protestant opinion would be united, or at least predominant, if it were not for the difference which exists as to the civil incapacities.

Thirdly – In the course of the last autumn, out of a regular infantry force in the United Kingdom, amounting to about 30,000 men, 25,000 men were stationed either in Ireland or on the west coast of England with a view to the maintenance of tranquillity in Ireland – this country being at peace with the whole world.

Fourthly – Though I have not the slightest apprehension of the result of civil commotion – though I believe it could be put down at once – yet I think the necessity of being constantly prepared for it while the Government is divided, and the two Houses of Parliament are divided, on the Catholic Question, is a much worse evil than its actual occurrence.

Fifthly – The state of political excitement in Ireland will soon render it almost impracticable to administer justice in cases in which political or religious considerations are involved. Trial by jury will not be a just or a safe tribunal, and, above all, not just nor safe in cases wherein the Government is a party.

These are practical and growing evils, for which I see no sufficient remedy if the present state of things is to continue; and the actual pressure is so great as fully to warrant, in my opinion, a recourse to other measures.

My advice therefore to His Majesty will be, not to grant the Catholic claims, or any part of them, precipitately and unadvisedly, but in the first instance to remove the barrier which prevents the consideration of the Catholic Question by the Cabinet – to permit his confidential servants to consider it in all its relations, on the same principles on which they consider any other great question of public policy, in the hope that some plan of adjustment can be proposed, on the authority and responsibility of a Government likely to command the assent of Parliament, and to unite in its support a powerful weight of Protestant opinion, from a conviction that it is a settlement equitable towards the Roman Catholics, and safe as it concerns the Protestant Establishment.

ROBERT PEEL

Peel *Memoirs*, i.284-94

8   The Catholic Emancipation Act, 1829

The technical exclusion of Roman Catholics from parliament derived from the compulsory oaths of allegiance and supremacy, as reformulated at the Revolution, which denied the spiritual and ecclesiastical supremacy of foreign princes and prelates, and from the compulsory declaration against transubstantiation, the invocation of saints and the sacrifice of the Mass. The oaths of allegiance and supremacy which could be required from parliamentary electors also operated as a theoretical, if not necessarily as an actual, bar to the exercise of the franchise by Roman Catholics in England, though by an act of 1794 the omission of the oaths was permitted unless demanded by the candidates. In Ireland Roman Catholics had since 1793 been allowed to vote for but not to sit in parliament. Roman Catholics had also been excluded from civil office and in England from commissions in the armed forces (though there was considerable confusion about the state of the law with regard to the latter category) by the oaths of allegiance and supremacy. As can be seen, the act repealed these technical disqualifications and formally permitted Roman Catholics to sit in Parliament, vote at elections and hold civil and military office subject to the new compound oath which replaced for these purposes the old oaths of allegiance, supremacy and abjuration.

An Act for the Relief of His Majesty's Roman Catholic Subjects
[13 April 1829]

Whereas by various Acts of Parliament certain Restraints and Disabilities are imposed on the Roman Catholic Subjects of His Majesty, to which other Subjects of His Majesty are not liable : . . . And whereas by various Acts certain Oaths and certain Declarations . . . against Transubstantiation and the Invocation of Saints and the Sacrifice of the Mass, as practised in the Church of *Rome*, are or may be required to be taken, made, and subscribed by the Subjects of His Majesty, as Qualifications for sitting and voting in Parliament, and for the Enjoyment of certain Offices, Franchises, and Civil Rights : Be it enacted . . . That from and after the Commencement of this Act all such Parts of the said Acts . . . be and the same are (save as herein-after provided and excepted) hereby repealed.

II. . . . from and after the Commencement of this Act it shall be lawful for any Person professing the Roman Catholic Religion, being a Peer, or who shall after the Commencement of this Act be returned as a Member of the House of Commons, to sit and vote in either House of Parliament respectively, being in all other respects duly qualified to sit and vote therein, upon taking and subscribing the following Oath, instead of the Oaths of Allegiance, Supremacy, and Abjuration :

'I A.B. do sincerely promise and swear, That I will be faithful and bear true allegiance to his Majesty King *George* the Fourth, and will defend him to the utmost of my Power against all Conspiracies and Attempts whatever, which shall be made against his Person, Crown, or Dignity; and I will do my utmost Endeavour to disclose and make known to His Majesty, His Heirs and Successors, all Treasons and traitorous Conspiracies which may be formed against Him or Them : And I do faithfully promise to maintain, support, and defend, to the utmost of my Power, the Succession of the Crown, which Succession, by an Act, intituled *An Act for the further Limitation of the Crown, and better securing the Rights and Liberties of the Subject*, is and stands limited to the Princess *Sophia*, Electress of *Hanover*, and the Heirs of her Body, being Protestants; hereby utterly renouncing and abjuring any Obedience or Allegiance unto any other Person claiming or pretending a Right to the Crown of this Realm : And I do further declare, That it is not an Article of my Faith, and that I do renounce, reject, and abjure the Opinion, that Princes excommunicated or deprived by the Pope, or any other Authority of the See of *Rome*, may be deposed or murdered by their Subjects, or by any Person whatsoever: And I do declare, That I do not believe that the Pope of *Rome*, or any other Foreign Prince, Prelate, Person, State, or Potentate, hath or ought to have any Temporal or Civil Jurisdiction, Power, Superiority, or Pre-eminence, directly or indirectly, within this Realm. I do swear, That I will defend to the utmost of my Power the Settlement of Property within this Realm, as established by the Laws; And I do hereby disclaim, disavow, and solemnly abjure any Intention to subvert the present Church Establishment, as settled by Law within this Realm: And I do solemnly swear, That I never will exercise any Privilege to which I am or may become entitled, to disturb or weaken the Protestant Religion or Protestant Government in the United Kingdom: And I do solemnly, in the Presence of God, profess, testify, and declare, That I do make this Declaration, and every Part thereof, in the plain and ordinary Sense of the Words of this Oath, without any Evasion, Equivocation, or mental Reservation whatsoever.

So help me GOD.'

V. . . . it shall be lawful for Persons professing the Roman Catholic Religion to vote at Elections of Members to serve in Parliament for *England* and for *Ireland*, and also to vote at the Elections of Representative Peers of *Scotland* and of *Ireland*, and to be elected such Representative Peers, being in all other respects duly qualified, upon taking and subscribing the Oath herein-before appointed. . . .

X. . . . it shall be lawful for any of His Majesty's Subjects professing the Roman Catholic Religion to hold, exercise, and enjoy all Civil and Military Offices and Places of Trust or Profit under His Majesty, His Heirs or Successors, and to exercise any other Franchise or Civil Right, except as herein-after excepted, upon taking and subscribing, at the Times and in the Manner herein-after mentioned, the Oath herein-before appointed. . . .

XII. . . . nothing herein contained shall extend or be construed to extend to enable any Person or Persons professing the Roman Catholic Religion to hold or exercise the Office of Guardians and Justices of the United Kingdom, or of Regent of the United Kingdom, under whatever Name, Style, or Title such Office may be constituted; nor to enable any Person, otherwise than as he is now by Law enabled, to hold or enjoy the Office of Lord High Chancellor, Lord Keeper or Lord Commissioner of the great Seal of *Great Britain* or *Ireland*; or the

Office of Lord Lieutenant, or Lord Deputy, or other Chief Governor or Governors of *Ireland*; or His Majesty's High Commissioner to the General Assembly of the Church of *Scotland*.

XXIV. [Anglican titles of provinces, sees etc. not to be assumed by Roman Catholics.]

XXVII–XXXVII. [Clauses aimed at suppression of Jesuit and other religious orders other than female orders. Existing members of such orders and native members returning from abroad to register; no foreign members to be allowed into U.K. except under licence and for maximum of six months; no new members to be admitted into religious orders.]

Statutes (10 Geo. IV cap. 7)

II

PARLIAMENTARY REFORM, 1831-2

1 The Case for Reform

The government plan of reform was first revealed on 1 March 1831 when leave was sought to bring in a bill to amend the representation of England and Wales. Though the official leader of the House of Commons was Lord Althorp, the motion was entrusted to Lord John Russell who had been a member of the Committee of Four which drew up the draft bill for the cabinet and was therefore better acquainted with its details. A seven-night debate followed at the end of which the bill was allowed to be brought in without a division and given its first reading. The second reading was fixed for 21 March and after two nights of debate passed by 302 votes to 301 in the largest division ever known in British parliamentary history. The bill differed in many of its details from that which finally became law in 1832. In particular the proposal to reduce the size of the House of Commons from 658 members to 596 (see (a) below) aroused much opposition and it was a defeat on this issue in committee on 19 April which decided the government to withdraw the bill, dissolve parliament (22 April) and appeal to the electorate. The slender majority on the principle of the bill on the second reading had in fact made it almost certain that it would not be able to stand up to detailed criticism in committee.

(a) *Lord John Russell*, 1 March 1831

I come now to the utmost difficult part of this subject – the explanation of the measure, which, representing the King's Ministers, I am about to propose to the House. Those Ministers have thought, and, in my opinion justly, that it would not be sufficient to bring forward a measure which should merely lop off some disgusting excrescences, or cure some notorious defects; but would still leave the battle to be fought again with renewed and strengthened discontent. They have thought that no half measures would be sufficient – that no trifling, no paltering, with so great a question could give stability to the Throne – authority to the Parliament – or satisfaction to the Country. . .
The chief grievances of which the people complain are these; – First, the nomination of Members by individuals. Second, the Elections by close Corporations; third, the Expense of Elections. With regard to

the first – the nomination by individuals – it may be exercised in one of two ways; either over a place containing scarcely any inhabitants, and with a very extensive right of election, or over a place of wide extent and numerous population, but where the franchise is confined to very few residents. . . . We have addressed ourselves to both these evils, because we have thought it essential to apply a remedy to both; but they must, of course, be dealt with in different ways. With regard to Boroughs where there are scarcely any inhabitants, and where the elective franchise is such as to enable many individuals to give their voices in the choice of Members for this House, it would be evidently a mere farce to take away the right from the person exercising it, and to give it to the borough; and the only Reform that can be justly recommended is, to deprive the borough of its franchise altogether. . . . It would be a task of extreme difficulty to ascertain the exact proportion of the wealth, trade, extent, and population, of a given number of places, and we have, therefore, been governed by what is manifestly a public record – I mean the population returns of 1821, and we propose that every borough which in that year had less than 2,000 inhabitants, shall altogether lose the right of sending Members to Parliament. The effect will be, utterly to disfranchise sixty boroughs. But we do not stop here. . . . We find that there are forty-seven boroughs, of only 4,000 inhabitants, and these we shall deprive of the right of sending more than one Member to Parliament. We likewise intend that Weymouth, which at present sends four Members, shall, in future, only elect two. The abolition of sixty boroughs will occasion 119 vacancies, to which are to be added forty-seven for the boroughs allowed to send only one Member, and two of which Weymouth will be deprived, making in the whole 168 vacancies. Such is the extent to which Ministers propose to go in the way of disfranchisement. But, as I have already said, we do not mean to allow that the remaining boroughs should be in the hands of select Corporations – that is to say, in the possession of a small number of persons, to the exclusion of the great body of the inhabitants, who have property and interest in the place represented. . . . We therefore propose that the right of voting shall be given to householders paying rates for, or occupying a house of, the yearly value of £10. and upwards. Whether he be the proprietor, or whether he only rent the house, the person rated will have the franchise upon certain conditions hereafter to be named. At the same time, it is not intended to deprive the present electors of their privilege to vote, provided they be resident. With regard to non-residence, we are of the opinion that it produces much expense, that it is the cause of a great deal of bribery, and that it occasions such manifold and manifest evils, that electors who do not live in a place ought not to be permitted to retain their votes. At the same time, I do not believe that we are inflicting even upon this class any injury, for nearly all, either in one place or in another, will possess a franchise as belonging to the great mass of householders. With regard to resident voters, we propose that they shall retain their right during life, but that no vote shall be allowed hereafter, excepting on the condition. . . . I now beg leave to direct the attention of the House to that part of the plan which relates to the expense of long-protracted polls, and which, while it removes that evil, also greatly facilitates the collection of the sense of the elective body. The names of electors are to be enrolled, by which means we hope that the disputes regarding qualification will be in a great measure avoided. We propose that all electors in counties, cities, towns, or boroughs, shall be registered, and for this purpose, machinery will be put in motion very similar to that of the Jury Act: . . . These regulations are extremely simple, and will prevent all those vexatious and noisy scenes now so often witnessed, regarding disputed votes. The means of ascertaining who are the electors being made thus easy, there will be no reason why the poll should be kept open for eight days, or for a longer period; and it is proposed that, nearly according to the present law, booths shall be erected for the voters of the different parishes, so that the whole poll may be taken in two days. . . . With respect to the manner of proceeding at Elections, we have it in view to introduce a measure which can hardly fail to be an improvement of the present system. Everybody knows, and must have lamented the enormous expense to which candidates are put in bringing voters to the poll. An election in Yorkshire has been known to cost nearly £150,000; and in Devonshire some of the electors are obliged to travel forty miles over rough cross-roads, which occupies one day; the next is consumed in polling, and the third in returning home; the whole scheme being a manifest source of vast expense, and most inconvenient delay. We propose, therefore, that the poll shall be taken in separate districts, into which the counties are to be divided, those districts to be arranged according to circumstances by the Magistrates at Quarter Sessions. . . . Having gone through the several alterations proposed in England and Wales, in Scotland and Ireland, I now come to the result. The number of

Members now belonging to this House is	658
The number to be disfranchised	168
Number remaining	490

Additional Members for Scotland	5
Additional Members for Ireland	3
Additional Members for Wales	1
Additional Members for the metropolis	8
New Members for large towns in England	34
Additional Members for counties in England	55
Total additional Members	106
Members of the House not to be disfranchised	490
Total	596

Making a decrease of sixty-two Members in the total number of Representatives. I will now state the number of additional persons who, I suppose, will be entitled to votes for counties, towns, and boroughs under this Bill:

	Persons
The number in towns and boroughs in England already sending Members, will be increased by	110,000
The electors of towns (in England) sending Members for the first time I estimate at	50,000
Electors in London, who will obtain the right of voting	95,000
Increase of electors in Scotland	60,000
In Ireland, perhaps	40,000
Increase in the counties of England probably	100,000

It is my opinion, therefore, that the whole measure will add to the constituency of the Commons House of Parliament, about half a million of Persons, and these all connected with the property of the country, having a valuable stake amongst us, and deeply interested in our institutions. They are the persons on whom we can depend in any future struggle in which this nation may be engaged, and who will maintain and support Parliament and the Throne in carrying that struggle to a successful termination. I think that those measures will produce a further benefit to the people, by the great incitement which it will occasion to industry and good conduct. For when a man finds, that by industrious exertion, and by punctuality, he will entitle himself to a place in the list of voters, he will have an additional motive to improve his circumstances, and to preserve his character amongst his neighbours. I think, therefore, that in adding to the constituency, we

are providing for the moral as well as for the political improvement of
the country. . . .

(b) *Lord Palmerston*, 3 March 1831

There were some, he knew, who called the present Reform by the
name of Revolution. There were others, he believed, who thought
that it fell far short of what the people were entitled to demand; but he
was convinced that all educated and intelligent men, who admitted the
importance of preserving and consolidating the constitutional institutions, would be satisfied that the plan now proposed was well adapted
to the end which all had in view. Any man who looked at the workings
of the present system must see, that there were five great and peculiar
blemishes, which it was necessary to remove, in order to fit it for the
intelligence and feelings of the times in which we lived. The first of
these was the system of nomination by the patrons of boroughs; the
second, the gross and barefaced corruption which prevailed among the
lower classes, when their votes become necessary to the higher; the
third, the absence of all adequate balances of representation with
respect to the great manufacturing and commercial towns; the fourth,
the great expense of elections; and the fifth, the very unequal and unjust
distribution of the power of voting among the middle and lower
classes. The plan then before the House applied to all these defects, and
he was convinced that, if calmly and dispassionately examined, there
was not an evil they generated for which it did not provide a sure and
effectual remedy. . . . The object the Government had in view in
framing the Bill was, first, to give Representatives to the great manufacturing towns; next, to add to the respectability of the electors;
and then to increase the number of those who claim to enjoy the right
of choosing their Representatives. This had been done by conferring
the right of voting generally on those who inhabited a house paying
£10. a year rent. The independence, too, of the electors was secured by
throwing open the closed boroughs to the inhabitants of the surrounding parishes, increasing their numbers, and making it impossible for any
individual to control them. In making these alterations, the Ministers
disclaimed any intention to sever the ties which bind together the
middle classes and the aristocracy. On the contrary, it was their earnest
desire to increase, rather than to diminish, that influence – an influence
arising from good conduct and propriety of demeanour on the one side,
and respect and deference on the other; and which was as honourable

to those who exercised it, as to those who acknowledged its authority. The measure before the House was not intended to affect this power, for it gave additional reasons for supporting and defending it; but it was intended to destroy that corrupt influence which destroys all public principle, and debases the state of every class of society wherever it has existence. . . . There were many and strong objections to virtual representation, and they applied with great force to the manufacturing towns which were unrepresented, and the interests of which were seriously affected by almost all the measures that were discussed in Parliament. In fact, if there were any classes who required more than others proper Representatives, they were the inhabitants of large manufacturing towns – Representatives who understood their interests, and who might be ready to watch over them. For this purpose, the Government proposed to give thirty-six Members to the manufacturing towns; and because this was done, a cry had been raised that the balance between the agricultural and manufacturing interests was destroyed. But the plan proposed went to restore to the landed interest that influence which he thought indispensable to the safety and prosperity of the country, by giving fifty-five Members to the counties, and still further, by conferring votes on copyholders, and not permitting those who had votes for towns to enjoy the same privilege in counties. He looked, indeed, on the increase of the Members for counties as the surest and most stable basis of representation; for, without meaning to disparage the manufacturing or commercial interests, he must say, that he considered the soil to be the country itself. . . . The great merit of the Bill, in his opinion, was, that it altered the distribution of political power, and restored the Constitution, by placing the middle classes in that situation to which they were entitled, and which was most likely to prove advantageous to themselves and to the community.

Ibid., 1324-30

2   A Conservative Criticism

The general election of 1831 *(April)* resulted in a large majority in favour of reform and a second bill passed the House of Commons in September and went up to the Lords. There on 8 October it was defeated by 199 votes to 158, the news being greeted by widespread riots in the country, particularly at Derby and Nottingham, with some loss of life. Parliament was prorogued and reassembled for a new session in December when the government introduced a third reform bill, embodying a number of concessions including the maintenance of the existing numbers of the House of Commons. Peel's speech, from which an extract is given below, was made during the debate on the second reading of the bill, which produced a two to one majority in its favour.

Peel

I expected that the present ministers would bring in a reform bill on their acceptance of office; but I believe, in my conscience, that the concessions made by them to the popular demands have been far more extensive than was at all necessary. I was not prepared for so extravagant a measure, still less could I have thought that they would venture to bring in so large a measure of reform within three months after they had taken office, and while the country was yet agitated by the events of the French Revolution. No issue of this discussion can be satisfactory, for, decide as we may, there must be much irreparable evil. I may be obliged to submit by necessity to a plan of reform which I cannot successfully oppose; but believing, as I do, that the people of this country are grossly deceived, grossly deluded, in their expectations of the practical benefits they will derive from reform, I shall not be precluded from declaring my opinion, and opposing that reform as long as I can. My opinions being thus wholly opposed to ministers on the question of reform, I am precluded from taking any part whatever in the settlement of the question. I am satisfied with the constitution under which I have lived hitherto, which I believe is adapted to the wants and habits of the people, I deplore a disposition, which seems too prevalent, to innovate unnecessarily upon all the institutions of the country. I admit, that to serve the sovereign, and the public in an office of honour and dignity, is an object of honourable ambition; but I am ready to sacrifice that object, rather than incur the responsibility of advocating measures which, I believe on my conscience, will tend to the destruction of the best interests of the country. I will continue my opposition to the last, believing, as I do, that this is the first step, not directly to revolution, but to a series of changes which will affect the property, and totally change the character, of the mixed constitution of this country. I will oppose it to the last, convinced, that though my opposition will be unavailing, it will not be fruitless, because the opposition now made will oppose a bar to further concessions hereafter. If the whole of the House were now to join in giving way, it will have less power to resist future changes. On this ground I take my stand, not opposed to a well-considered reform of any of our institutions which need reform, but opposed to this reform in our constitution, because it tends to root up the feelings of respect, the feelings of habitual reverence and attachment, which are the only sure foundations of government. I will oppose to the last the undue encroachments of that democratic spirit to which we are advised to yield without resistance. We may make it supreme – we may establish a republic full of energy – splendid in talent – but in my conscience I believe fatal to our liberty, our security and our peace.

Peel, *Speeches*, ii.433

3   A Country-House in a State of Defence

The fourth Duke of Newcastle was a strong Tory and prominent opponent of the reform bill, who had already suffered from the attentions of the mob in London. When the news of the rejection of the bill by the House of Lords reached Nottingham, where there was much economic distress among the domestic handloom weavers in the stocking-making industry, rioting began and soon spread in the absence of any effective police-force or substantial body of military. Nottingham Castle, the property of the duke, though almost derelict and never inhabited by him, was ransacked and burnt down. The rioters then proceeded to further destruction and pillage in the surrounding countryside. The news reached the duke late on 12 October and he started out early the next morning for his great country-house at Clumber in north Nottinghamshire. Of the sons mentioned in the account who had taken charge of the defence measures, Lord Lincoln (the future politician and cabinet minister) was then aged twenty, Charles and Thomas, his twin younger brothers, were eighteen.

I reached Clumber about eleven o'clock, having met videttes of yeomanry patrolling within two miles of the house. On my arrival at the house the garrison expressed their rejoicing and welcome by loud and long-continued cheers. In the house I found my dear Lincoln, Charles, and Thomas, with the officers of the troop stationed here. . . . I could not believe that I was at Clumber; the whole was changed, everything removed that was valuable, such as pictures, ornaments, furniture, statues, etc., etc., and nothing but bare walls, and the house filled with men in all the rooms, with cannons (of which I have ten three-pounders and fourteen little ship guns), fire-arms, muskets and pistols and sabres, planted in their proper positions and in all the windows. . . . The preparations are indeed formidable. . . . In the house there are two hundred men, and out of it a great many more, including a troop of yeomanry of seventy men and horses. . . .

I would not give any orders last night, not wishing without full deliberation to alter anything that Lincoln had done; but this morning I determined to make a change in our mode of defence. I therefore settled that the yeomanry should be dismissed, all but a sergeant and

twelve men, whom I kept until the next morning. I reduced the
number of men to twenty picked men, who have been nearly all old
soldiers. I admit none of them into the house. I have made a barrack for
them in the offices adjoining, where they sleep and mess, and I mount
a chain of sentries in a ring round the house. . . . At night I went to see
that all my arrangements were carried properly into execution, and
found them well done. On my return home, from not knowing the
counter-sign, I was taken prisoner by one of my own sentries. We
shall soon be altogether and comfortable again. I have heard of no
fresh aggressions.

> The Duke of Newcastle's Diary, 13-14
> October 1831, from J. Martineau, *Life of
> Henry Pelham, Fifth Duke of Newcastle* (1908),
> pp. 33-4

4 The House of Lords and Reform

The third reform bill passed the Commons in March 1832. When it went up
to the Lords it received, with the help of moderate Tories (the Waverers), a
small majority of 9 on the second reading. After the Easter recess, however, the
opposition carried (7 May) an amendment in committee postponing the dis-
franchising clauses of the bill. Grey informed the king that the cabinet would
resign unless they were empowered to create at least fifty peers to ensure the
passage of the bill and the king accepted their resignation on 9 May. By 15 May
it was clear that Wellington would be unable to form an administration and
that nobody else was prepared to do so. It was not, however, until 18 May (the
day after the debate from which the extracts below are taken) that the king ended
the crisis by agreeing to make enough peers to guarantee the safety of the bill.
The following extracts illustrate the opposed points of view on the constitutional issue. The one additional comment on Grey's statement of what has
become the accepted modern view is that whereas the dissolution of the House
of Commons by ministers is an appeal to a third party, namely the electorate,
the creation of fresh peers is an act of ministers themselves, who are thus both
judge and jury in their own cause. As against this, the general election of 1831
had clearly given the cabinet in the modern phrase a 'mandate' to pass a reform
bill.

(a) Duke of Wellington

Ministers found, in the course of last Session, that there was a large
majority in this House against the principle of the Reform Bill. Now,
my Lords, what is the ordinary course for a Minister, under such
circumstances, to pursue? My Lords, it is, to alter the measure – to

endeavour to make it more palatable to that branch of the Legislature which is opposed to it. But, in this case, the Minister says 'no, I will next Session bring in a Bill as efficient as that which has been just rejected.' And what did the Minister do? My Lords, I have no hesitation in saying that, notwithstanding the opposition of this House, he brought in a measure stronger and worse than any one of the measures before introduced; and this measure he wished to force through the House by a large creation of Peers. How many Peers it is not necessary to state; it is enough to say, a sufficient number to force it through the House. It is only necessary for me to state the proposition. If this be a legal and constitutional course of conduct – if such projects can be carried into execution by a Minister of the Crown with impunity, there is no doubt that the Constitution of this House and of this country is at an end. I ask, my Lords, is there anybody blind enough not to see that if a Minister can, with impunity, advise his Sovereign to such an unconstitutional exercise of his prerogative as to thereby decide all questions in this House, there is absolutely an end put to the power and objects of deliberation in this House – an end to all just and proper means of decision. I say, then, my lords, thinking as I do, it was my duty to counsel his Majesty to resist this advice. And, my Lords, my opinion is, that the threat of carrying this measure of creating Peers into execution, if it should have the effect of inducing noble Lords to absent themselves from the House, or to adopt any particular line of conduct, is just as bad as its execution: for, my Lords, it does by violence force a decision on this House, and on a subject, my Lords, on which this House is not disposed to give such a decision.

Hansard, xii.994–9

(b) Earl Grey

It is not necessary to go into this long-disputed question of Reform. The Bill, when it was brought forward, received the general approbation of the country, such as no former measure had ever yet commanded. . . . It passed the House of Commons, after an appeal to the country, by a triumphant majority. Most unfortunately it was rejected by this House. Another Bill, as efficient as this, the noble Duke says, was brought in; but that it is more dangerous I dispute and deny: it had the good fortune to receive the sanction to its principles of a majority of your Lordships on the second reading. I now come to the point which conduced to the present state of affairs. I had hoped that it would pass the Committee without such a change as would render it impossible for me to consent to its being sent down to the other House;

but, on the very first clause, a motion was made, the result of which was
described as trifling and unimportant; but, in my opinion, it proved
such a disposition in this House, and was essentially of such injury to the
Bill, that I felt I should not be justified in going further. . . . It was then
for me to consider which of two courses I would pursue – whether I
would abandon the Bill altogether, or whether I would recommend
that measure to his Majesty which could alone enable the Government
to go on with the Bill. We adopted the latter alternative, and did
propose to His Majesty that advice which the noble Duke has arraigned
so severely. . . . We had either to recommend this measure, with all
the risk of consequences, or suffer this House to come into collision with
public opinion and the other House of Parliament – a collision to which,
if this House were unwise enough to commit itself, it is not easy to
suppose that it can be victorious. . . . Now I say that, under these
circumstances, the advice to create new Peers was required. The noble
and learned Lord says, that it was not constitutional; but I say that it
was constitutional, and I can refer him to books of authority on that
subject, in which it is distinctly asserted, that one of the uses of vesting
the prerogative of creating new Peers in the Crown is, to prevent the
possibility of the recurrence of those evils which must otherwise result
from a permanent collision between the two Houses of Parliament;
and this danger was rendered imminent by the opposition made to the
Reform Bill by the noble Lords on the other side of the House. And,
I ask, what would be the consequences if we were to suppose that such
a prerogative did not exist, or could not be constitutionally exercised?
The Commons have a control over the power of the Crown by the
privilege, in extreme cases, of refusing the Supplies; and the Crown has,
by means of its power to dissolve the House of Commons, a control
upon any violent and rash proceedings on the part of the Commons;
but if a majority of this House is to have the power, whenever they
please, of opposing the declared and decided wishes both of the Crown
and the people, without any means of modifying that power, then this
country is placed entirely under the influence of an uncontrollable
oligarchy.

Ibid., 1004-6 (17 May 1832)

5   A Warning to the Cabinet

Between 15 and 18 May the future of the bill was still in doubt. Discussions
between the whig cabinet and the king were inconclusive; an expected declara-

tion from leading Tory peers that they would desist from opposing the bill had not materialised; there was still a genuine reluctance on the part of the prime minister and some of his colleagues to proceed to a mass creation of new peers; and statements by ministerial and opposition spokesmen in parliament gave the public no clear picture of what was happening. Since 11 May there had been regular consultations in London between members of the Political Union and deputations from the Birmingham and other provincial political unions on the best means of organising a national civil resistance in the event of a Wellington ministry. There was to be a meeting of the cabinet on 18 May and J. C. Hobhouse, secretary at war and a radical Whig, asked Francis Place, the leading spirit in the political unions, to write him a letter which could be placed before his colleagues. The document reproduced below was in response to that request and was clearly designed to stiffen the determination of the cabinet to stay in office by a graphic description of the consequences if they did not. At the cabinet meeting it was decided to insist on a pledge from the king to make peers as the only security for the success of the bill. Armed with a cabinet minute to that effect Lord Grey and the Chancellor, Lord Brougham, finally secured the king's promise to make sufficient peers to carry the bill. This was announced in both Houses the same evening.

May 18, 1832. 9 A.M. Dear Sir John, – The moment it was known that Earl Grey had been sent for, the *demand for gold ceased*. No more placards were posted, and all seemed to be going on well at once. Proof positive this of the cool courage and admirable discipline of the people. We cannot, however, go on thus *beyond to-day*. If doubt remain until to-morrow, alarm will commence again, and panic will follow. No effort to *stop the Duke by going for gold* was made beyond a mere demonstration, and you saw the consequences. What can be done in this way has now been clearly ascertained, and if new efforts must be made, they will not be made in vain.

Lists containing the names, addresses, &c., of all persons in every part of the country likely to be useful have been made, the name of every man who has at any public meeting shown himself friendly to reform has been registered. Addresses and proclamations to the people have been sketched, and printed copies will, if need be, be sent to every such person all over the kingdom. Means have been devised to placard towns and villages, to circulate hand-bills, and to assemble the people. So many men of known character, civil and *military*, have entered heartily into the scheme, that their names when published will produce great effect in every desirable way. If the Duke comes into power now, we shall be unable longer to 'hold to the laws'; break them we must, be the consequences whatever they may; and we know that all must join with us to save their property, no matter what may be their

private opinions. Towns will be barricaded, new municipal arrangements will be made by the inhabitants, and the first town which is
barricaded shuts up all the banks. 'Go for Gold,' it is said, will produce dreadful evils. We know it will, but it will prevent other evils
being added to them. It will *stop the Duke*. Let the Duke take office as
Premier, and we shall have a commotion in the nature of a civil war,
with money at our command. If we obtain the money, he cannot get it.
If it be but once dispersed, he cannot collect it. If we have money we
shall have the power to feed and lead the people, and in less than five
days we shall have the soldiers with us.

G. Wallas, *Life of Francis Place* (1918), pp.
315-16

6   The Reform Act of 1832

Most text-books for the period summarise the main provisions of the reform
act. A few special points may be noticed here.

(1) A large proportion of pre-1832 voters continued to enjoy their old
franchise. In the counties the historic 40/- freeholder was not disturbed. Even if
his property lay within a borough boundary he remained a county elector
unless otherwise qualified for the borough franchise. In the old boroughs which
still returned members after the act the ancient franchises also remained intact
during the life-time of their possessors and subject to residence.

(2) Two features of the act in particular were not in accordance with the real
wishes of the cabinet:

(a) the retention of the freemen, a notoriously corrupt class of voter, in the
boroughs

(b) the enfranchisement of the £50 tenant-at-will in the counties (cl. XX).
This was the so-called Chandos clause (from the name of its mover, Lord
Chandos) which received support not only from country gentry anxious
to strengthen landlord and agricultural interests but also from radicals
favouring any extension of the suffrage. It was probably the government's defeat on this issue which prompted them to insist on the retention
of the county vote by the urban 40/- freeholder since this especially in
the populous areas would offset the effect of the Chandos clause.

(3) A number of provisions were designed to keep down expenses of elections
and diminish disorder and riot, notably the limitation of the poll to two days
(cll. LXII, LXVII) the division of large constituencies into separate polling
districts (cl. LXIII, and the institution of electoral registers with provision for
annual revision before special courts (cll. XXXVII, XLI, XLIX, L). The introduction of annual registration as a qualification for voting provided an unin-
tended stimulus to electoral organisation in the constituencies which was a
powerful factor in the growth of party activity during the next decade.

(4) Separate reform acts were passed in 1832 with differing sets of provisions for Scotland (2 & 3 Will. IV cap. 65), and Ireland (cap. 88). The changes effected were greater in Scotland where the franchise had been extremely limited, than in Ireland where the Union Act of 1800 and an act accompanying Catholic Emancipation in 1829 had already made major changes. In 1800 most of the small Irish boroughs had been disfranchised and in 1829 the county freehold franchise had been raised from 40/- to £10.

An Act to amend the Representation of the People in *England* and *Wales*
[7 June 1832]

Whereas it is expedient to take effectual Measures for correcting divers Abuses that have long prevailed in the Choice of Members to serve in the Commons House of Parliament, to deprive many inconsiderable Places of the Right of returning Members, to grant such Privilege to large, populous, and wealthy Towns, to increase the Number of Knights of the Shire, to extend the Elective Franchise to many of His Majesty's Subjects who have not heretofore enjoyed the same, and to diminish the Expense of Elections; be it therefore enacted. . . . That each of the Boroughs enumerated in the Schedule marked (A) to this Act annexed, (that is to say,) *Old Sarum, Newtown, St. Michael's or Midshall, Gatton, Bramber, Bossiney, Dunwich, Ludgershall, St. Mawe's, Beeralston, West Looe, St. Germain's, Newport, Blechingley, Aldborough, Camelford, Hindon, East Looe, Corfe Castle, Great Bedwin, Yarmouth, Queensborough, Castle Riding, East Grinstead, Higham Ferrers, Wendover, Weobly, Winchelsea, Tregony, Haslemere, Saltash, Orford, Callington, Newton, Ilchester, Boroughshire, Stockbridge, New Romney, Hedon, Plympton, Seaford, Heytesbury, Steyning, Whitchurch, Wootton Bassett, Downton, Fowey, Milborne Port, Aldeburgh, Minehead, Bishop's Castle, Okehampton, Appleby, Lostwithiel, Brackley,* and *Amersham,* shall from and after the End of this present Parliament cease to return any Member or Members to serve in Parliament.

II. . . . each of the Boroughs enumerated in the Schedule marked (B.) to this Act annexed, (that is to say,) *Petersfield, Ashburton, Eye, Westbury, Wareham, Midhurst, Woodstock, Wilton, Malmesbury, Liskeard, Reigate, Hythe, Droitwich, Lyme Regis, Launceston, Shaftesbury, Thirsk, Christchurch, Horsham, Great Grimsby, Calne, Arundel, St. Ives, Rye, Clitheroe, Morpeth, Helston, North Allerton, Wallingford,* and *Dartmouth,* shall from and after the End of this present Parliament return One Member and no more to serve in Parliament.

III. . . . each of the Places named in the Schedule marked (C.) to this Act annexed, (that is to say,) *Manchester, Birmingham, Leeds, Greenwich,*

Sheffield *Sunderland, Devonport, Wolverhampton, Tower Hamlets, Finsbury Mary-le-bone, Lambeth, Bolton, Bradford, Blackburn, Brighton, Halifax, Macclesfield, Oldham, Stockport, Stoke-upon-Trent,* and *Stroud* ... shall from and after the End of this present Parliament return Two Members to serve in Parliament.

IV. ... each of the Places named in the Schedule marked (D.) to this Act annexed, (that is to say), *Ashton-under-Lyne, Bury, Chatham, Cheltenham, Dudley, Frome, Gateshead, Huddersfield, Kidderminster, Kendal, Rochdale, Salford, South Shields, Tynemouth, Wakefield, Walsall, Warrington, Whitby, Whitehaven,* and *Merthyr Tydvil* ... shall from and after the End of this present Parliament return One Member to serve in Parliament. ...

XII. ... in all future Parliaments there shall be Six Knights of the Shire, instead of Four, to serve for the County of *York,* (that is to say,) Two Knights for each of the Three Ridings of the said County. ...

XIII. ... in all future Parliaments there shall be Four Knights of the Shire, instead of Two, to serve for the County of Lincoln, (that is to say,) Two for the Parts of *Lindsey* in the said County, and Two for the Parts of *Kesteven* and *Holland.* ...

XIV. ... each of the Counties enumerated in the Schedule marked (F.) to this Act annexed shall be divided into Two Divisions, which Divisions shall be settled and described by an Act to be passed for that Purpose in this present Parliament ... and that in all future Parliaments there shall be ... Two knights of the Shire for each Division of the said Counties. ...

XV. ... in all future Parliaments there shall be Three Knights of the Shire, instead of Two, to serve for each of the Counties enumerated in the Schedule marked (F. 2) to this Act annexed, and Two Knights of the Shire, instead of One, to serve for each of the Counties of *Carmarthen, Denbigh,* and *Glamorgan.* ...

XVI. ... the *Isle of Wight* in the County of *Southampton* shall for the Purposes of this Act be a County of itself ... and shall return One Knight of the Shire to serve in every future Parliament. ...

XVIII. ... no Person shall be entitled to vote in the Election of a Knight or Knights of the Shire to serve in any future Parliament, or in the Election of a Member or Members to serve in any future Parliament for any City or Town being a County of itself, in respect of any Freehold Lands or Tenements ... except such Person shall be in the actual and *bonâ fide* Occupation of such Lands or Tenements, or except the same shall have come to such Person by Marriage, Marriage Settlement, Devise, or Promotion to any Benefice or to any Office, or except the same shall be of the clear yearly Value of not less than Ten Pounds. . . .

XIX. . . . every Male Person of full Age, and not subject to any legal Incapacity, who shall be seised at Law or in Equity of any Lands or Tenements of Copyhold or any other Tenure whatever except Freehold . . . of the clear yearly Value of not less than Ten Pounds . . . shall be entitled to vote in the Election of a Knight or Knights of the Shire to serve in any future Parliament for the County, or for the Riding, Parts, or Division of the County, in which such Lands or Tenements shall be respectively situate. . . .

XX. [Holders of sixty-year leases for lands or tenements of not less than £10 clear annual value, or of twenty-year leases of not less than £50 clear annual value, and tenants of lands or tenements liable to a yearly rent of not less than £50, to qualify as voters for county elections.]

XXIV, XXV. [Persons with property qualifications for a borough franchise not to qualify for the county franchise by reason of the same property whether or not they have actually acquired the right to vote for the borough.]

XXVII. . . . in every City or Borough which shall return a Member or Members to serve in any future Parliament, every Male Person of full Age, and not subject to any legal Incapacity, who shall occupy . . . as Owner or Tenant, any House, Warehouse, Counting-house, Shop, or other Building, being, either separately, or jointly with any Land within such City, Borough, or Place occupied therewith by him as Owner, or occupied therewith by him as Tenant under the same Landlord, of the clear yearly Value of not less than Ten Pounds, shall, if duly registered according to the Provisions herein-after contained, be entitled to vote in the Election of a Member or Members to serve in any future Parliament for such City or Borough. . . . [Registration to be conditional on previous occupation for at least twelve months, residence for at least six months within seven miles, and payment of rates and assessed taxes in respect of the qualifying property.]

XXXVII. And whereas it is expedient to form a Register of all Persons entitled to vote in the Election of a Knight or Knights of the Shire to serve in any future Parliament . . . the Overseers of the Poor of every Parish and Township shall on the Twentieth Day of *June* in the present and in every succeeding Year cause to be fixed on or near the Doors of all the Churches and Chapels within such Parish or Township, or . . . in some public and conspicuous Situation within the same respectively, a Notice . . . requiring all Persons who may be entitled to vote . . . in respect of any Property situate wholly or in part in such

Parish or Township, to deliver or transmit to the said Overseers on or before the twentieth Day of *July* in the present and in every succeeding Year a Notice of their Claim as such Voters. . . .

XXXVIII. . . . the Overseers of the Poor of every Parish and Township shall on or before the last Day of *July* in the present Year make out or cause to be made out, . . . an alphabetical List of all Persons who shall claim as aforesaid to be inserted in such List as Voters . . . and . . . before the last Day of *July* in every succeeding Year make out or cause to be made out a like List, containing the Names of all Persons who shall be upon the Register for the Time being as such Voters, and also the Names of all Persons who shall claim as aforesaid to be inserted in such last-mentioned List as such Voters. . . .

XLI. . . . the Lord Chief Justice of the Court of King's Bench . . . for *Middlesex* and the Senior Judge for the Time being in the Commission of Assize for every other County shall . . . nominate and appoint for every such County . . . or Divisions of such County, a Barrister or Barristers to revise the Lists of Voters in the Election of a Knight or Knights of the Shire; and such Barrister or Barristers . . . shall give public Notice, . . . of the several Times and Places at which he or they will hold Courts for that Purpose, such Times being between the Fifteenth Day of *September* inclusive and the Twenty-fifth Day of *October* inclusive in the present and in every succeeding Year, and he or they shall hold open Courts for that Purpose at the Times and Places so to be announced. . . .

XLIV-L. Similar provisions for the preparation of lists of voters in cities and boroughs, appointment of revising barristers, and revision of electoral lists.

LXII. . . . at every contested Election of a Knight or Knights to serve in any future Parliament for any County, or for any Riding, Parts, or Division of a County, the polling shall commence at Nine o'Clock in the Forenoon of the next Day but Two after the Day fixed for the Election, unless such next Day but Two shall be *Saturday* or *Sunday*, and then on the *Monday* following, . . . and such polling shall continue for Two Days only.

LXIII. . . . the respective Counties in *England* and *Wales*, and the respective Ridings, Parts, and Divisions of Counties, shall be divided into convenient Districts for polling . . . provided that no County, nor any Riding, Parts, or Division of a County, shall have more than Fifteen Districts and respective Places appointed for taking the Poll.

LXVII. [Similar provisions as in LXII for limiting the poll in cities and boroughs to two days.]

SCHEDULE (F.)
COUNTIES to be Divided

Cheshire
Cornwall
Cumberland
Derbyshire
Devonshire
Durham
Essex
Gloucestershire
Kent
Hampshire
Lancashire
Leicestershire
Norfolk

Northumberland
Northamptonshire
Nottinghamshire
Shropshire
Somersetshire
Staffordshire
Suffolk
Surrey
Sussex
Warwickshire
Wiltshire
Worcestershire

SCHEDULE (F.2.)
COUNTIES to return Three Members each

Berkshire
Buckinghamshire
Cambridgeshire
Dorsetshire

Herefordshire
Hertfordshire
Oxfordshire

Statutes 2 & 3 Will. IV cap. 45

7 Electoral Morality in the Reformed Era

Bribery, corruption, intimidation and various forms of illegitimate influence continued after 1832 and a number of parliamentary committees were set up in an attempt to remedy a situation for which responsibility was shared by both candidates and electors. But the ultimate decision in disputed election cases lay with House of Commons committees who tended to vote on party lines and there was often a vested interest in concealing facts from an enquiry. As a result the sporadic legislation passed between the first and second reform acts to purify elections had little effect. Joseph Parkes, some of whose evidence before a committee of 1835 is given below, was one of the most experienced election agents of the day. A Birmingham solicitor by training and a radical liberal in opinion, he had played an important part as intermediary between the government and the Political Unions in 1832 and later became the most trusted electoral expert of the Liberal party.

I consider that almost every place has a system of corruption peculiar to itself, where the same end is obtained, and the same system of corrupt practices prevail, but in different modes; I have seen many gentlemen openly pay down agreed sums, and before the poll, and I have been privy, that is I have had a personal knowledge: generally speaking, the bribery is contracted to be done after the expiration of the period for petitioning; I am now confining my observations to direct money bribery, but which of course I do not consider to be the only species of bribery; money's worth is equally bribery.... I mentioned to the Committee, that peculiar customs prevail in particular towns; some towns are particularly free from certain practices of corruption, and other towns from other practices. I never heard in my life of a bribed voter at Warwick, till the election of 1831, though a native of Warwick, and present at many elections, and the demoralising effect of it was most lamentable when once commenced. I heard it insinuated to have taken place in 1831, I am not sure that it was practised then, but in 1832 it was most openly practised....

Have you observed a perceptible difference in the morality of the town since that practice commenced? – Very great indeed, from bribery and other corrupt expenditure of money, and also in the state of society...

I should say that all parties in Warwick, before the contest under the Reform Bill, lived on very amicable terms, both the higher and the lower classes in the town. It is scarcely credible what has subsequently been the effect of party spirit among all classes of society, even between gentlemen and the lower classes, and the consequences have also been most injurious to shopkeepers. The customers extensively transferred their custom, and the tradesmen complain that the wealthy landed proprietors and gentry in the neighbourhood have left them and gone to others; to a certain extent I should think both parties have practically resorted to very exclusive dealing, and all parties, more or less, suffered in their custom. Indeed I know that no prominent member of either party, generally speaking, would have now any dealings with men of opposite party principles; I know that intimate personal friends, and men who used to meet at the same table, are now on hostile terms, and that they speak one of another in language exceedingly disgraceful and very lamentable....

Do you conceive it to be consequent on the introduction of direct bribery? – Not consequent on the introduction of bribery alone, but resulting from the whole system of treating, and the election petition presented to expose the corruption, and the legal proceedings afterwards instituted. . . .

With regard to the question of threats and intimidation, and corrupt influence of that species, will you describe that which has come under your observation? – That class of influence is most extensive, and in many instances, of most pernicious operation, equally in counties as towns; I believe that it occasions a most fraudulent exercise of the franchise, and to a very great extent.

Take counties in the first instance, describe the class of persons on whom it operates? – In counties the smaller freeholders are naturally very much under the influence of those on whom they are dependent for their subsistence, and of course the tenants are extremely dependent.

The master over the labourer? – Yes; and the clergymen I know to have most extensive influence in many places.

A minister over a congregation, whether dissenting or otherwise? – Unquestionably; of course I am not now confining myself to any party allusion.

The creditor over the debtor? – It applies so much to the tenantry that the poll book is almost a topography of the estates, and it is irrational to suppose, whatever the reasonable or the proper influence of the landlord over the tenantry, that their political opinions are so extremely similar, as in the case of 30 tenants that the whole shall go with the landlord.

Have you known a case in which, from the change of politics on the part of the landlord, the tenantry have voted differently on one election from what they did on the election immediately previous? – I have known the most remarkable instances; I have known a landlord correspond with a candidate on the subject of the corn laws, and I have known him send a list of the whole of his tenants, and that he should come with them and vote one way or the other, according to the explanation he received from the candidate. . . .

Is it a common thing for a candidate to ask permission of a landlord to canvass his tenants? – It is, ordinarily. I do not consider it always an act of propriety to canvass amongst the tenants of a landlord on either side, and particularly my own side, without having the landowner's leave, and it is a common practice for us to write to request leave to canvass them. . . .

P. P. 1835 viii (Report on Bribery at Elections), Evidence 1597-1739

III

CHURCH AND DISSENT, 1832-47

1 An Indignant Dissenter

In March 1833 the Deputies of the Three Denominations, otherwise known as the Protestant Dissenting Deputies (a London Committee which looked after the national interests of Presbyterians, Congregationalists and Baptists), set up a United Committee 'to consider the grievances under which Dissenters now labour, with a view to their Redress'. In May the United Committee (consisting of the Committee of Deputies, delegates from the Body of Ministers, the Protestant Society and others) drew up a list of six specific grievances on which they wished the government to take action. But a deputation to the prime minister failed to secure satisfaction and it was clear that pressure would have to be exerted if results were to be obtained. There was the further fear that the royal commission set up in 1832 to enquire into ecclesiastical revenues might result in legislation to reform the Church, leaving the question of Dissenting grievances on one side. The Congregationalist George Hadfield, writer of the following letter, was an author and politician, later M. P. for Sheffield 1852-74. He had edited reports for the Charity Commission in 1829, stood unsuccessfully as liberal candidate for Bradford in 1835 and took part in the formation of the Anti-Corn Law League.

Sir,

(Dec 1833)

It is a matter of the deepest regret and surprise that no steps are taking by the Dissenters in England, at this critical juncture, to assert their principles and claim their just rights, when it is generally understood that his Majesty's ministers, or at least the majority of them, will concede nothing to us which they can possibly avoid; and that they intend to bring forward, next session, their plan of church reform, the tendency of which will be decidedly unfavourable to our interests, and will consolidate the political power and influence of one dominant sect. . . .

If, then, we owed Earl Grey and his colleagues any debt of gratitude, for doing us an act of justice before they took office, in getting the Test Laws repealed, we have now paid it; and it is time to look to our own interests, in which are involved the best interests of the country.

We are required to submit to the domination of a corrupt state church; to be governed by bishops; to see 3,5000,000£. at the least (but more likely 5,00,000£.) annually expended in the maintenance of a clergy, of whom a vast majority do not preach the gospel; to see the cure of souls bought and sold in open market; to have the Universities closed against us, and all the iniquities of those degraded places continued; to be taxed, tithed, and rated to the support of a system which we abjure; to be compelled to submit to objectionable rites and ceremonies at marriage, baptism, and burial; – in one word, to be left out of the social compact, and degraded. . . . We have hitherto demanded too little; and, consequently, we have been refused everything worth caring about. The bill for relieving places of worship from the poor-rates, which was the fruit of the labours of the last session of Parliament, is no boon to us. It applies to churches in the establishment more than to ourselves, and I doubt much whether it will save the Dissenters 50£. a year. I fear we have even misled the Government itself by asking for trifles, when we ought to have been contending for great principles. What signifies a small church-rate, when we should be contending against a corrupt state church? What is the trifling amount of poor-rates levied upon a very few of our chapels, in comparison of millions of pounds annually expended on a secular and dominant clergy? – and all this is done in a country burdened with a debt which grinds us all! The real points at issue between the Government and us are very few, and may soon be stated. They are chiefly as follow, viz: –

1st. A total disconnexion between church and state, leaving the details consequent thereupon to be dealt with by Parliament.

2nd. The repeal of the Act of Charles II., which enables bishops to sit in the House of Lords.

3rd. The repeal of all laws which grant compulsory powers to raise money for the support of any church whatever.

4th. The reformation of the Universities, the repeal of all religious tests, and a grant of equal rights in them.

5th. A reformation of the laws relating to marriage and registration with equal rights in places of public burial.

No Government whatever could long resist any of these just and reasonable requirements, if perseveringly demanded; and it is well known that several members of the present administration would gladly and promptly grant all of them. . . . Our political power is far more justly estimated by our opponents than by ourselves, and few of the members of Parliament would venture to be indifferent or opposed to our wishes. Lord Durham knows us well, and his advice is particularly applicable to us: 'The power rests with yourselves, now, to instruct your representatives *as to the measures which you*, the respectability and intelligence of the country, *have set your hearts on, and they will inevitably be carried.*'

I am, Sir,

Your very obedient servant,

George Hadfield

> *Baptist Magazine* (3 ser.), xxv.597-600 (Dec. 1833)

2   Dissenting Agitation Continued

With growing Dissenting agitation the government made unsuccessful attempts in the 1834 session to meet some of their demands. Two bills – one to transfer the burden of church rates to the land-tax, the other to allow marriages in dissenting chapels subject to banns being called in the parish church – were abandoned in the face of dissenting criticism. A private bill actively supported by several ministers to admit dissenters to degrees at Oxford and Cambridge was defeated in the House of Lords. The parliamentary and Anglican opposition encountered had the effect of hardening Dissenting temper. Public meetings were held in many large towns and there was criticism of the United Committee for its cautious tactics. In May a joint meeting of the Committee and country delegates took the extreme step of accepting in principle the separation of Church and State, i.e. disestablishment as a basis of policy; though this had not been one of the six points put forward by the United Committee a year earlier. Edward Baines sen., liberal M.P. for Leeds (1834-41) was a leading Dissenter and proprietor of the *Leeds Mercury*.

At a meeting for Conference between the United Committee appointed to obtain the redress of the grievances of dissenters, and deputies from various parts of the country, summoned specially for the purpose held at the City of London Tavern, on Thursday, May 8, 1834; Edward Baines, Esq., M.P., in the chair;

It was resolved,

1. That this meeting recognizes the great and leading principle of full and complete separation of church and state as the true basis on which equal rights and justice can be secured to all classes of His Majesty's subjects.

2. That this meeting cannot but express their deep regret that the reasonable expectations of dissenters, founded on the admission, by His Majesty's ministers, of the justice of their claims, and on the repeated assurance of a desire on their part to grant relief, have been frustrated by Lord John Russell's Dissenters' Marriage Bill, and by

Lord Althorp's propositions respecting church-rates, – the only measures which the government have hitherto introduced into parliament for the relief of dissenters.

3. That this meeting concurs in the objections which have been made by the united committee to the marriage bill, and especially to the propositions respecting church-rates, which they consider fallacious and altogether unsatisfactory, inasmuch as, while they change the name, they prolong the duration of a burden, from which dissenters have already, in many parishes, procured either partial or entire relief, and also gives new energy to a principle against which they have strongly protested as impolitic and unjust.

4. That this meeting entertains a full conviction that the English episcopal church possesses in the property now at her disposal, and in the wealth of her individual members, resources abundantly adequate to defray all the expenses of upholding the edifices in which her members worship; and feels entitled to claim the entire abolition of all imposts for that purpose, upon the same principles of expediency and justice which induced parliament to abolish Church-cess in Ireland.

5. That the individuals now present, acquiescing in the declaration made by one of His Majesty's ministers, that it is a grievance for any class of religious professors to be taxed for the support of a church to which they do not belong, engage to take all constitutional measures to oppose the adoption of the proposed plan respecting church-rates, and to secure the perfect enjoyment of their religious rights.

6. That a deputation from this meeting wait on Lord Althorp, to communicate their sentiments relative to the measure which his Lordship has introduced concerning church-rates. . . .

7. That the deputation report the result of their interview with Lord Althorp to the United Committee.

8. That this meeting recommends the formation of Voluntary Church Societies in London, and throughout the country, for the purpose of diffusing the great principles maintained by such associations among the inhabitants of the United Kingdom.

9. That the deputies now present will take immediate measures for personally communicating with the members of parliament for their respective counties, cities and boroughs, upon the respective resolutions passed this day, and that they report the result to the United Committee.

10. That the most cordial thanks of this meeting be given to the United Committee for their valuable and efficient public services, and that they be requested to continue the same.

11. That the deputies from the country, now present, undertake to

interest themselves in their respective districts to procure contributions to meet the expenses incurred by the United Committee in prosecuting the important objects of their formation; and that the monies so collected be remitted to the secretary, on account of the treasurer of that committee.

Baptist Magazine, xxvi.255 (June 1834)

3   An Indignant Anglican

Two parallel sets of events in 1834,

(a) Dissenting agitation, the abortive government relief bills, the call for disestablishment, and such isolated incidents as a motion in the House of Commons for the exclusion of bishops from the House of Lords which secured 58 votes;

(b) Ward's motion (May) for the appropriation of part of the revenues of the Irish Church (since 1800 legally united with the Church of England), the recourse by the government to a commission of enquiry and the consequent resignation of Stanley, Graham and two other members of the government,

had made the position of the Established Church the great controversial issue of the session.

The letter below expresses the fears of many Anglicans that a planned attack was being made on the whole position of the Church. The motion for exclusion of bishops was made by C. Rippon, M.P. for Gateshead (one of the new Reform Act boroughs), seconded by W. D. Gillon, Presbyterian member for Falkirk boroughs, and supported by many radical and Irish members.

Three of the great embankments of our constitution have recently been cut through. – one in 1828, another in 1829, and a third in 1831. The first broke down the long-established qualification for office in our Christian state; the second *let in*, as *legislators*, men implacably hostile to the great living principle of all our institutions; and third, as a natural consequence of the two former, poured into the House of Common (to use the Hollander's term) an '*overstrooming*' of the turbid waters of sheer *mammonry*, democracy, and republicanism. The professed object of all these changes has been to *liberalise* our institutions; or, in other words, to obliterate what are called all INVIDIOUS *distinctions*. The consequences of these vital changes in our constitution are daily manifesting themselves in the necessary laxity and (so called) *popularity* of public measures, which actually leaves all the great interests of society in a state of instability and insecurity. I am sure that no man, who has watched the progress of these disorganizing principles, was in the slightest degree astonished at Mr Rippon's motion, on the 13th of March, to bring in 'a bill to *relieve*' (observe the sarcastic malignity of the term!) 'the arch-bishops and bishops of the established church from the exercise of their legislative and judicial functions in the House of Peers'.... Mr Rippon, the mover, and member for *Gateshead*, described his motion as 'the first step ('the little whimble') towards a *full and fair* discussion of the church establishment'; and, in the plenitude of his candour, observed, that 'the state of the community was such as to demand a reform in the established church, to make it *conformable* and afford *satisfaction* to an ENLIGHTENED people'. This reform he would have made *in time*, while it may be 'considered *a boon*, and *possibly* not extorted as a matter of right'.... Mr Harvey told the house that 'there was a *principle* and a *cause* AT WORK out of doors, which, at no distant time, would make it a question, not whether the bishops should continue to sit in the House of Lords, but whether the establishment should be maintained *at all*'. He was also kind and generous enough to think, that, 'if *we* were to disrobe the church to-morrow of its *gorgeous array*, and to deprive the bishops of their overgrown temporalities, the church, as a *Christian church*, would still *not only stand*, but *flourish*'. It seems the bishops 'belie the simplicity of the creed they profess, and arm infidelity by the *gorgeousness* of their worldly appearance'. 'He would send the bishops to those *scenes of moral simplicity* where the example of their lives might excite *confidence* in *their flock* and lead them to a *due observance* of the precepts of religion.' In other words, he would make them parish priests, and live up to their religion. The suggestion is as ingenious as it is charitable! 'All that the non-conformists required was, that religion should be let to stand upon *its own inherent* and imperishable *pretensions*'; i.e., voluntary contributions, or Franciscan beggary. Here is the clue to the whole outcry!

Mr Hume thought 'the bishops had made themselves *odious* to *three-fourths* of the people of England, by the manner in which they had INTERFERED in the proceedings on the Reform Bill'. Yet he adds, 'they had a *right* to give their opinions'; but, as they were so wilful and wrong-headed as to use that right in opposition to persons so religious and conservative as Mr Hume, 'they should be removed from a spot where their political functions interfered with their other duties'....

Such are the precious fruits of a spurious *liberality*, which would be popular by the concession of even vital points. How far it may be allowed to proceed, rests, under Heaven, with those to whom the destinies of this degraded country are committed. Let us remember the declaration of Lord Grey, in the House of Lords, on Friday, the 22nd day of March:- 'His wish, he again repeated, was to go *every length* he conscientiously could in removing the real grievances of the dissenters. He professed himself to be the *sincere* and *ardent* well-wisher to their claims.' 'GRIEVANCE', like 'emancipation' and 'reform', is now the cant term, the 'argumentum breve' et 'ad misericordiam', the broad cloak for arrogancy and encroachment!

British Magazine, vi.273-8 (Sept. 1834)
Correspondence

4 Church Reform: The Ecclesiastical Commission of 1835

One of Peel's main preoccupations when taking office in 1834 was to allay the hostility to the Church not merely by remedying some of the Dissenters' grievances (in which he did not succeed) but also by setting up machinery for a real and substantial reform of the Church. The royal commission appointed by Grey in 1832 to enquire into church revenues had been a fact-finding body without any policy implications. The Ecclesiastical Commission established by Peel in February 1835 was intended to uncover defects, propose remedies to the legislature, and supervise their administration. Its composition, which included strong episcopal and ministerial representation, was designed to make its recommendations acceptable both to parliament and the Church. The following letter to a sympathetic liberal Conservative peer (one of the Waverers of 1832) illustrates Peel's general views on the immediate task before the Commission. When the Whigs returned to office they renewed the Commission (June 1835) with the substitution of Whig for Conservative ministerial members and in 1836 it was put on a permanent statutory basis, as the 'Ecclesiastical Commissioners for England'.

(Confidential)
Whitehall, January 12, 1835

MY DEAR LORD HARROWBY,

I hope that the deep interest which you have uniformly taken in the real welfare of the Church will induce you to lend a favourable ear to my present proposal.

I am convinced of the absolute necessity of taking some effectual and practical step with a view not only to the satisfaction of the public mind, but to the higher object of promoting the spiritual efficiency of the Church, and the great moral and religious purposes for which the Church was founded.

I feel it my solemn duty as a Minister, and as a member of the Church, to advise the Crown to administer its Church patronage from this time forth on a new principle, and calmly and dispassionately to consider, as great preferments fall vacant, whether there may not be some appropriation of the revenues of those preferments better calculated to serve the cause of religion than an exact adherence to the existing law and long observed usage in respect to those revenues. The best way to illustrate my meaning and intentions is to take a practical case.

If the Bishopric of Ely were to fall vacant tomorrow, I should advise the Crown not to make an immediate appointment to it, but to consider these several particulars:

The amount of the revenues of the See, and the propriety of appropriating only a part of those revenues to the support (the decorous, nay the liberal support) of the Episcopal station: The expediency of making some new distribution of Episcopal duties between the Bishopric of Ely and adjoining or neighbouring Bishoprics, which are comparatively overloaded with functions which might be annexed to Ely: Lastly, a review of the livings within the diocese, and especially of those at the disposal of the Bishop, with a view to appropriate the superfluous revenues of the See to their increase, in cases wherein the existing provision should be notoriously inadequate to ensure a resident minister. . . . I should look again to the provision of Episcopal duties in the North of England; and if I, and those real friends of the Church with whom I should be most anxious to consult, should be (as I am confident we should be) of opinion that the altered circumstances of the times – the state of public feeling – the spiritual interests of the Establishment – required the application of a new principle, I should at once advise the Crown to consent to its application.

Amidst the harassing duties in which I have been lately engaged, and which, to say the truth, have up to this time left me but little leisure to consider any other matters than those immediately connected with the formation of the Government, this subject has chiefly occupied my anxious attention. I have had much confidential communication with the Archbishop of Canterbury and the Bishop of London, and I have the satisfaction of finding on their part an earnest desire to lend me their assistance, and the support of their authority in doing something effectual in Church reform, in the encouraging and (where possible) the compulsion of residence – the prevention of improper pluralities – the gradual extirpation of sinecures in the Church.

The immediate course I propose to pursue for the purpose of laying the safe foundations at least of progressive reform in the Church, is the appointment of a Commission to which I should confidentially refer, on the avoidance of any great preferment, the consideration of those arrangements in detail which might best promote the object I have in view, and which Commission might also consider prospectively the arrangements which it might be advisable to adopt, either with the consent of those who have at present existing interests, or, if their consent cannot be had, on the occurrence of a vacancy.

I think of constituting the Commission thus: –

The Archbishop of Canterbury	The Lord Chancellor
The Archbishop of York	Sir Robert Peel
The Bishop of London	Mr Goulburn
The Bishop of Lincoln	Mr Charles Wynn
The Bishop of Gloucester	Sir Herbert Jenner;

and, with your permission, yourself.

I will only repeat that I earnestly hope that your general concurrence in the views of which I have given the outline, and your devotion to the real interests of religion and the Church, may induce you to give me on this Commission the inestimable value of your sanction and co-operation.

Believe me, &c.,

Robert Peel

Peel *Memoirs*, ii.72-5

5 The Whig Educational Scheme of 1839

In 1833 the government had started an annual parliamentary grant of £20,000 for education to be administered through the two great voluntary societies, the Anglican National Society and the Dissenting British and Foreign Society. The inadequacies of the system and the unequal allocation of the grant between the two societies led to criticism and by 1838 the government was under pressure from radical and liberal supporters to exert a greater measure of state control. The Whig scheme put forward in stages during 1839 provided for

(a) the establishment of a Committee of the Privy Council to supervise the distribution of an increased educational grant with a system of state inspection for schools benefiting from it.

(b) the abandonment of the policy of making state grants only when a comparable amount was raised from voluntary sources (a system which gave an advantage to the Anglicans).

(c) the institution of 'normal' (i.e. teacher training) schools under state inspection and on a non-confessional basis with provision for general (i.e. collective) as well as special (i.e. denominational) religious instruction.

The scheme was in general welcomed by Dissenters as a large step towards religious equality.

The lords of the committee recommend by their report, that the sum of 10,000l. granted by parliament in 1835 towards the erection of normal or model schools be given in equal proportions to the national society and the British and Foreign school society. That the remainder of the subsequent grants of the years 1837 and 1838 yet unappropriated, and any grant that may be voted in the present year, be chiefly applied in aid of subscriptions for buildings, and in particular cases for the support of schools connected with these societies; but that the rule hitherto adopted of making a grant to those places where the largest proportion is subscribed, be not invariably adhered to, should applications be made from very poor and populous districts, where subscriptions to a sufficient amount cannot be obtained.

The committee do not feel themselves precluded from making grants in particular cases, which shall appear to them to call for the aid of government, although the application may not come from either of the two mentioned societies.

The committee are of opinion that the most useful applications of any sums voted by parliament would consist in the employment of those monies in the establishment of a normal school under the direction of the state, and not placed under the management of a voluntary society. The committee, however, experience so much difficulty in reconciling conflicting views respecting the provisions which they are desirous to make in furtherance of your majesty's wish that the children and teachers instructed in this school should be duly trained in the principles of the christian religion, while the rights of conscience should be respected, that it is not in the power of the committee to mature a plan for the accomplishment of this design without further consideration, and they therefore postpone taking any steps for this purpose until greater concurrence of opinion is found to prevail.

The committee recommend that no further grant be made now or hereafter for the establishment or support of normal schools, or of any other schools, unless the right of inspection be retained in order to secure a conformity to the regulations and discipline established in the several schools with such improvements as may from time to time be suggested by the committee. A part of any grant voted in the present year may be usefully applied to the purposes of inspection, and to the means of acquiring a complete knowledge of the present state of education in England and Wales.

Annual Register, 1839, pp. 141-2

6 Anglican Views on National Education

Anglican fear of an attack on the Church's educational system started several years before 1839, largely as a result of the activities of the radical Central Education Society founded in 1836 which advocated a national educational system with democratic control of schools and state inspectors. Its leading figure were its founder, Sir Thomas Wyse, M.P. for Waterford, R. A. Slaney, M.P. for Shrewsbury, Lord Brougham, and J. A. Roebuck, M.P. for Bath 1832-7 and 1841-7. In June 1838 Wyse's motion in the House of Commons for a mixed Board of Commissioners to administer the parliamentary grant was nearly carried despite government opposition. The reaction of young Conservative Anglican politicians like T. D. Acland, W. E. Gladstone, W. M. Praed, Lord Sandon and Lord Ashley, encouraged by Peel, was to work through the National Society for the establishment of diocesan training colleges and more Church secondary schools. The extract at (a) is from a pamphlet published by Acland in January 1839. The resolution printed in (b) was passed at a meeting of the National Society which had been carefully organised by Acland and his friends as a demonstration of Anglican strength. The extreme claim on behalf of the Church that it had the right of superintending national education was not one however which Peel endorsed and in the debate on the government's resolutions in June he merely argued that no system of national education should be approved which excluded the Established Church.

(a) An Anglican Politician   *(Acland - Jan 1839)*

Mr Wyse, Lord Brougham, and Mr Slaney, differ widely in their views. . . . But though they differ thus widely as to the kind of schools in which they propose that the people should be educated, they are all agreed upon one point – viz., that the first object to be aimed at is to obtain a commission or board of education under the control of Parliament and having the disposal of public money. . . . Whether it is likely the present government will appoint a commission is a question into which it is not proposed to enter now; that strong pressure has been exerted to force them into the measure is certain. . . . The decision of the question probably hangs on the use which the Church makes of every moment's delay which may be granted to her exertions. . . . We are grateful for the hair-breadth escapes of last session, and willing to exert ourselves during the interval which will precede the next. . . . No London committee can compete with an organized method of attack such as is now pursued, but the energies of the Church in her several dioceses may suffice to our need. And let it be remembered that mere politicians always support the most powerful body; only let the strength of the Church be felt in acts, not in words. . . . It may yet be proved by God's blessing that the only truly national system of education is the Catholic system of the Church.

> *National Education, The Present State of the Question Elucidated,* January 1839 [by T.D.A.], quoted in *Sir Thomas Acland Memoir & Letters* (1902), ed. A. H. D. Acland, pp. 86-7

(b) Resolution of the National Society, 28 May 1839

At the great meeting of the National Society presided over by the Archbishop of Canterbury it was resolved: 'That it is an object of the highest national importance to provide that instruction in the truths and precepts of Christianity should form an essential part of every system of education intended for the people at large, and that such instruction should be under the superintendence of the clergy and in conformity with the doctrines of the Church of this realm as the recognized teacher of religion.'

> *Ibid.,* p. 91, note

7   A Dissenting Protest against Anglican Claims

The intense Anglican public and parliamentary opposition to the 1839 scheme obliged the government to give way on several major points. The unpopular Normal School project was abandoned at an early stage and after prolonged negotiations the government agreed in 1840 to appoint inspectors only with the approval of the diocesan bishops and to revert to the old system of allotting educational grants in proportion to voluntary subscriptions. The concessions were felt by many Dissenters to be a defeat and began a steady movement of Dissenting opinion away from the idea of a state system and back to the old voluntary principle. At the same time the powers and pretensions of the Church demonstrated in 1839 further inflamed sectarian animosity. The hostility and defensiveness exhibited in the resolution printed below which marked the Dissenting attitude towards the Established Church in the early years of Victoria's reign were given further expression by various developments in the next few years: the Religious Freedom Society (1839), the *Nonconformist Weekly* founded (1841) to promote disestablishment, and the Anti-State Church Association (1844).

For the General Body of Dissenting Ministers see **I, 1** above. The Rev. John Hoppus was Congregational minister at Carter Street Chapel, London, and professor of philosophy and logic at University College, London University, since 1829.

RESOLUTIONS OF THE GENERAL BODY OF DISSENTING MINISTERS

At a special meeting, held at the Congregational Library, Finsbury, of the Three Denominations, in and about the Cities of London and Westminster, on the 6th of March, 1840, the Rev. Professor Hoppus, Doc. Phios. in the Chair, the following resolutions were unanimously adopted:-

National Education

IV. That the number of petitions presented of late to both Houses of Parliament, declaring the established clergy to be the persons in whom the superintendence of any system of national education should be mainly vested, exhibit an attempt to revive a long obsolete branch of priestly power, betraying a spirit as arrogant as it is unjust, and that should be resisted to the utmost, not only by the Protestant Dissenter, but by every friend to general liberty; that, as a matter of expediency, we should regard the placing of a system of that nature in such hands as tending rather to perpetuate than to remove the popular ignorance, discontent and irreligion, and as adapted to strengthen every prejudice unfavourable to our intelligence, virtue, and greatness, as a people: that, on the ground of justice, we are no less convinced that if any portion of the public money be granted for such purposes, it should be for the advancement of that secular education concerning which all are agreed, and not for education in religion, on which we are so much divided, and which, in such cases, will be best provided for in being left to the judgment of persons locally interested in school management: that we accordingly hail with peculiar satisfaction the fixed resolution evinced by her Majesty's Ministers to proceed upon these principles in the application of the late grant for this object.

Congregational Magazine (N.S.), iv.263-5 (1840)

8 Graham's Factory Education Scheme, 1843

When the Conservative ministry took office in 1841, the new Home Secretary, Sir James Graham, began to prepare a scheme for the better education of children in industrial areas. Since 1839 it seemed essential to win the approval of the Church for any state plan of education and in negotiations during 1842 Graham made several modifications to meet Anglican views. The scheme presented to Parliament in 1843 as part of a larger factory bill provided for the compulsory education of children in factories with a schoolmaster appointed on the nomination of the diocesan bishop and a school-board on which there would be a practical majority of Anglicans. There was strong and widespread Dissenting agitation against the scheme in which the Methodists (who had supported the Church in 1839) now joined. Various concessions by Graham failed to allay the excitement. Many Churchmen themselves began to feel lukewarm about the measure and no solid support for it was forthcoming from Anglican quarters. Despite support from prominent men on both sides of the House, Graham in the end withdrew the bill as unworkable even if passed in view of the hostility it would encounter. Lord Ashley was one of many who believed that much of the resistance to the scheme was due to the unpopularity of the Oxford Tractarian Movement led by Pusey and Newman which was widely thought to be leading the Church towards a form of Roman Catholicism.

(a) Sir Robert Peel to the Queen   June 16, 1843

In consequence of the persevering and general opposition of the Dissenting Body to the proposed measure of the Government for providing combined scriptural education for the children employed in factories, and the little prospect that they would, even if the Bill were carried, unite in giving effect to it, your Majesty's servants thought it better to withdraw the measure than make an attempt to carry it, which, as success depended upon general concord and goodwill, must be ultimately unavailing, and the progress of which must infallibly embitter religious animosity and strife.

C. S. Parker, *Sir Robert Peel* (1899), ii.561

(b) Lord Ashley to Sir Robert Peel   June 17, 1843

You might have carried your Bill through the House by unwilling voters and small majorities, but you could not have carried it into practical operation. Your difficulties would have been less from the fierceness and determination of the Dissenters and Wesleyans than from the utter coldness and apathy of the Church, both lay and ecclesiastical. Not a hundred men would have been found to introduce and support the system.

We must ascribe much – very much – of this resistance to the fears of the people caused and stimulated by the perilous pranks of Dr Pusey and his disciples. A vast body of Churchmen actuated by these alarms rejoiced in the opposition.

The clergy are not to be blamed for their backwardness. The Church has never made so great concessions: *they went to the very verge of what a man of principle could vote for*, but she made them in the hope of conciliation. We cannot be surprised that she should be reluctant to force a measure on the country which would not pacify their opponents and was distasteful to themselves.

Let this last trial be taken as a sufficient proof that 'united education' is an impossibility. It ought never again to be attempted. The Dissenters and the Church have each laid down their limits which they will not pass; and there is no power than can either force, persuade, or delude them.

Your Government has nothing to regret, except the loss of a healing measure. You would have much to regret had you not propounded it. But you have endeavoured to remove a great evil, and in so doing have thrown the responsibility, before God and man, on the shoulders and consciences of others.

Brit. Mus. Add. MSS. 40483 fo. 114

9 National Education: The Failure of a Policy

Though industrial disorder between 1837 and 1843 convinced Peel and Graham of the need for further education especially in the industrial areas, it was clear after the failure of Graham's factory plan that any scheme for national education would break down on the hostility between Church and Dissent. Similarly, though Peel when he became prime minister in 1841 was urged by Anglicans to obtain a parliamentary grant for the building and endowment of more parish churches (Church Extension), he was convinced that the time had passed when the legislature could ask the general taxpayer to contribute to the strengthening of one particular denomination. All he did was to pass in 1843 an act authorising the Ecclesiastical Commissioners to set up new parishes and provide stipends from existing church revenues. On the other hand many Dissenters, after the events of 1839 and 1843, feared that any further state control would mean either an extension of the influence of the Established Church or a purely secular form of education. Three years later the proposals of the Whig government in 1843 for changes in the administration of educational grants, involving an increase in state inspection and more professional training for teachers, led to a breach between the Whigs and their traditional Dissenting supporters at the general election of 1847. Edward Baines jun., the editor of the *Leeds Mercury*, was one of the chief spokesmen of the purely Voluntary school who opposed all state intervention in the field of education.

(a) Sir James Graham to Sir Robert Peel, 17 September 1843

own to you that I am afraid of an inquiry by a Commission into the want of moral and religious instruction in the manufacturing districts which have been recently disturbed.

I have no doubt that a frightful case might be clearly established of brutal ignorance and heathenish irreligion, and that it is the paramount duty of the Government to apply a progressive remedy to an evil of such magnitude and danger.

But if you issue a Commission, you will excite to the utmost the hopes and fears of rival factions. The truth will be shown in a light probably somewhat exaggerated, and the Government which exposes to view so great a national deformity ought to be prepared with an adequate remedy.

When we have proved the want of education, the need of pastoral care, the insufficiency of church room, what hope is there that we can agree in Parliament on a scheme of national instruction, or obtain funds for the building and endowment of new churches, on a scale commensurate with the necessity which we shall have established?

The religious differences which divide the three portions of the United Kingdom preclude the hope that any large drain on the public revenue for the purpose of extending the exclusive doctrine and discipline of the Church of England would be permitted.

By judicious measures we may gradually propagate the saving knowledge of Christian truth; we may diffuse the blessings of a scriptural education; we may render the property of the Church more available for sacred uses, and less subservient to temporal interests. All this may be done gently, almost silently, and from time to time public aid may be obtained. But if we appoint a Commission of Inquiry, if reports of striking effect be produced, and if, relying on these reports, we attempt any large measure, general alarm will be excited, a spirit of resistance will be generated, failure will ensue, and the good which might otherwise be effected will be rendered impossible.

Let me beg of you to consider this view of the subject before we decide on an inquiry.

C. S. Parker, *Sir James Graham* (1907), i.346

(b) Edward Baines jun. of Leeds

The adjourned Meeting of the Thirteenth Annual Assembly of the Congregational Union of England and Wales, was held at Leeds, on the 10th, 11th, 12th, and 13th days of October, 1843.

[11 October: debate on general education]

On the whole, we must admit two important facts, neither of them satisfactory to us as a religious denomination: viz. first, that there is a great deficiency, both in the quantity and quality of general education; and second, that dissenters have not done their share in supplying this great want. The practical questions that are suggested by these facts are, first, How is the admitted want of general education to be supplied? and second, What is *our* peculiar duty in regard to it? On the first point, the answer returned by a host of eminent statesmen and writers, by the example of other countries, and even by popular opinion in our own, amounting altogether to a mass of authority which it is really fearful of confronting, is, that it is the *duty of government* to supply the defect. ... I will, if the meeting will indulge me, state with all brevity, the result of the best consideration I have been able to give to the subject. I am compelled, then, to declare my opinion, that it is *not* the province of a government to educate the people; and that the admission of the principle that that *is* its province, would lead to practical consequences fatal to civil and religious liberty. The subject is too wide to be discussed at length, but I would respectfully suggest a few considerations in support of the view which I have taken. They are these: first, that the proper province of government is to make and administer laws, to protect person and property, and to conduct the external relations of a country; but that it is *not* its province to train the mind and morals of the people any more than it is to supply them with food, or to govern their families. Second, that if we grant it to be the province of government to educate the people, we must on the same principle grant that government ought to provide for the religious instruction of the people, – which admits the whole principle of state establishments of religion; and also to provide for the future supply of their intellectual wants, – which involves a censorship of the press. Third, that if it be the province of government to educate the people, it must be at once its right and its duty to do all that is requisite for that end, – which involves a direct or indirect control over all the machinery of education, over the systems of tuition, over the teachers, over the school books, over the raising and administering of the funds, over the parents and the children, and the employers of labour. It involves both *compulsion and prohibition*, and the enforcing of both by the only instrument which the civil power can wield, namely, fines and penalties. Fourth, that therefore the consistent carrying out of the principle, that it is the province of government to educate the people, would reduce the people of this country to a state of pupilage as complete as that of the people of

Prussia, or even of China; it would annihilate freedom of education, freedom of the press, freedom of conscience, and freedom of industry. Fifth, that it would interpose the most serious obstacles in the way of improvements in education, as is shown by the history of the endowed schools. Sixth, that it would put into the hands of government an enormous amount of patronage, which would assuredly be used for party and corrupt purposes, and which would endanger public liberty. There are those who would shrink from the idea of entrusting the education of the whole people to government, who yet think it right for government to provide for the education of the poor. But if the principle be once admitted, that it is the province of the government to educate any portion of the people, I do not see how we could stop short till it had the entire work in its own hands.

Congregational   Magazine   (N.S.),   vii.829–36
(1843)

IV

PARTIES AND POLITICS, 1832-47

1 Reform after the Reform Act: a Radical View

Although the Reform Act was designed by the government to be a measure of political pacification and its sweeping provisions (compared with earlier reform proposals) justified on those grounds, their Radical supporters expected the act to inaugurate a series of legislative reforms. Cobbett's *Manchester Lectures*, delivered in December 1831 on the assumption that parliamentary reform was now a certainty, elaborated thirteen propositions as a basis for legislation after the reform act passed. They included a revision of all pensions and the reduction of official salaries; the abolition of the army except for coastal artillery; the assumption of the defence of the country by the county militia; the abolition of tithe; the confiscation and sale of episcopal and cathedral property and crown lands, the proceeds to pay off the National Debt; the abolition of all internal taxes except the land-tax; the institution of a property tax; and the abolition of the Church of Ireland hierarchy.

A great many people mistake the Reform Bill for reform itself; and a very great mistake it is. The Reform Bill furnishes the means of making the reform. A reform means a *change for the better*; and, in this case, the change must be very great to be of any use at all. A great many people seem to imagine, or at least they act as if they imagined, that the mere sound of reform would be sufficient, without any proceedings to produce a change in the state of the country. The Ministers themselves appear to be amongst these persons; for you never hear from their lips any-thing seeming to indicate that they look upon it as necessary that some great change should take place in the manner of managing the affairs of the country. Yet, if some great change do not take place, in this respect, I am perfectly convinced that the passing of the Reform Bill would lead to disappointment and discontent, such as must plunge the country into utter confusion. Does any one believe that the mere sound of the word *Reform* will quiet the country? That, when the trader, who feels the work of ruin still proceeding, is told, in order to pacify him, not to complain *now*, for that we have *got reform*: does any one think, that that will make him submit to his ruin without further complaint? When the hungry and angry half-starved labourers complain of their sufferings, and are ready to break out into acts of violence; will they be quieted by telling them, that they must not complain *now*, for that we have *got reform*; will they, at the sound of that word, cease to harbour vindictive thoughts relative to those whom they deem their oppressors? Oh, no! the reform must be something more than *a bill*, something more than a bit of printed paper, it must, to be productive of harmony, cause something to be done to *better the state of the people*; and, in order to do this, it must produce, and quickly too, not only a change in the management of the affairs of the country, *but a very great change....*

If the *Reform Bill* be to leave the system of sway that which it now is; if the same sort of management of our affairs be to go on after that bill shall have passed as is going on now; and really, to judge from the language of the Ministers, one would say that *they contemplate no change*; if the *tithes* and *taxes* be still to remain such as they are; if a Bourbon gendarmerie be still to dog our steps, and stop us when they like at any hour of the day and night; if the Englishmen, who do all the work, be still doomed to live on potatoes and water, while those who take from them the fruit of their labour, are living on all the choice products of the earth; if Englishmen and women be still harnessed and made to draw like beasts of burden; if a reformed Parliament cannot find the means of protecting the *dead bodies* of the working poor, while such ample means are found for protecting the dead body of a *hare*, a pheasant, or a partridge; then, indeed, the bishops did right in opposing the Reform Bill; for a greater delusion, a greater fraud, never was attempted, to be practised on any part of mankind.

William Cobbett's *Manchester Lectures* (1832), pp. 8-9

2 The Reform Ministry after the Reform Act: A Government Defence

The wide and sometimes unrealistic expectations caused by the Reform Act were disappointed once the ministry settled down to the task of governing the country. Although the general election of 1832, the first under the new act, had produced an overwhelming 'Reform' majority, the government early realised that it was not a party majority pledged to its support and that criticism and opposition were as much to be expected from reformers as from the official opposition. At the end of the first session of the reformed parliament the ministry took the unusual step of publishing a pamphlet in defence of their administrative and legislative record. It was edited by D. Le Marchant, private secretary to the Lord Chancellor, Lord Brougham, with contributions from various departmental ministers. Appearing in September soon after prorogation, it had an immediate success and ran through four editions in a fortnight.

(1833)

It is the fortune of the present Government to be encountered by two hostile factions, the Tories and the Radicals, who appear to agree in no principle either of preservation or destruction, and have no object common to both, except that of endeavouring to persuade the people of the imbecility of the Ministers. . . .

But it must be remembered that the present Ministers are invested with the highest trust which it ever fell to the lot of men to execute. Their junction with either of the adverse parties must be fatal to the quiet of the country, and defeat, for a long period, all the good we have obtained, or may expect.

They must trust to the good sense of the great body of their fellow-citizens, to permit them gradually and steadily to repair the injuries which the country has sustained by a misgovernment of nearly fifty years, and claim a confidence for integrity for the future, by an impartial review of what has already passed.

The present Ministry wisely commenced the work of general reform by a reform in the constituency of the House of Commons. And surely, in effecting this great measure, no party can accuse them of want of integrity, or courage. They demolished by this blow the groundwork which had supported all preceding administrations. – All that for which former parties contended, and for which they sought to be in place. – With this reform, patronage, the main lever of former politicians, inevitably perished, and has left the present Ministers, as it will leave all future administrations, dependent solely on the support of the people. Their enemies did not then accuse them of doing nothing. The Tories announced the value of the measure by their terror, and the Radicals by their joy. As compared with the great measure of Reform, all others appear subordinate. The impression it created, the excitement it produced, still agitates the public mind. Its magnitude conceals the importance of all other political measures. Every step which has followed it appears diminutive, when compared with this mighty stride. It renders men dissatisfied with the delay required for the details of inferior changes, with which the welfare of large masses of the community is interwoven, and which cannot be carried into execution without great precaution or great injustice. . . .

That the present is a strong administration, no one can doubt who looks at its overwhelming majorities; if it have been too humble in the exercise of its strength, if it have paid an undue degree of attention to the suggestions of friends or even of enemies, it has been guilty of an error which may be easily pardoned, since experience shews that it is one not likely to be repeated. But we do not believe that any such error has been committed. We believe that such a reproach can be made only by those who do not understand the times in which they live, and who apply to the present constitution the traditions of one that has ceased to exist. When the House of Commons consisted of partisans, when every speech and vote was part of a system, when measures were introduced not because they were useful but because they were plausible, and opposed not because they were likely to do harm to the country, but lest they should do good to their proposers, – it might be the duty of a Government living in such an atmosphere of selfishness and insincerity, to form its plans in silence, and to carry them through with obstinacy, well knowing that what was good would be most likely to be attacked, and that whatever was proposed as an amendment was probably designed to be mischievous.

To get rid of this wretched system was the great object of the Reform Bill: and it *has* been got rid of. A majority of the Members of the House of Commons are partisans not of the Ministry or of the Opposition, but of good government. – And ought their warnings to be disregarded? Ought the voice of those who speak in the name of the whole people to have no more weight than if they were a body of mere nominees? Or laying aside what ought to be done, can this be done? Who doubts that it cannot? Who doubts that the willingness with which the present administration has listened to suggestions, the earnestness with which it has sought, in every quarter, and by every means, for information, the frankness with which it has not only allowed but forwarded every inquiry, must be imitated, and it cannot well be surpassed, by all who succeed them in the high office of presiding over the deliberations of a Reformed House of Commons?

Pamphlet: *The Reform Ministry and the Reformed Parliament* (1833)

3   The Tamworth Manifesto

The ministerial changes in 1834, the Irish Church policy of the government, and finally, the succession of Lord Althorp to his father's peerage and his proposed replacement as Leader of the House of Commons by Lord John Russell, induced the king to dismiss the Whig ministry in November 1834. Arriving back from Italy over three weeks later Peel had no option but to accept office. It was obvious that the small Conservative party in the Commons could not provide the basis for an administration and that a general election must be held. There was a general feeling in Conservative circles that some public announcement of the principles of the new administration was essential if the electorate was to be persuaded to give it a trial. It was an unprecedented action on the part of a government and there was considerable discussion on the best method to adopt: a speech by Peel at the Mansion House, a letter to his supporters in parliament, or a reply to an address from a specific group of M.P.s. In the end Peel decided to employ the orthodox medium of an address to his constituents at Tamworth. First appearing in the national press on 18 December it was at once recognised as an appeal to the country at large. Essentially the document was an electioneering weapon and contained a declaration not so much on Conservative principles in the abstract as of immediate attitudes towards the main political issues of the day. Much of what Peel said in it, he had said before. Nevertheless the circumstances in which it was issued made it an intellectual landmark in the growth of Conservatism after the Reform Act.

To the Electors of the Borough of Tamworth   (Dec. 1834)

Gentlemen,

On the 26th of November last, being then at Rome, I received from His Majesty a summons, wholly unforeseen and unexpected by me, to return to England without delay, for the purpose of assisting His Majesty in the formation of a new Government. . . .

My acceptance of the first office in the Government terminates, for the present my political connection with you. In seeking the renewal of it, whenever you shall be called upon to perform the duty of electing a representative in Parliament, I feel it incumbent upon me to enter into a declaration of my views of public policy, as full and unreserved as I can make it, consistently with my duty as a Minister of the Crown. . . .

I gladly avail myself also of this, a legitimate opportunity, of making a more public appeal – of addressing, through you, to that great and intelligent class of society of which you are a portion, and a fair and unexceptionable representative – to that class which is much less interested in the contentions of party, than in the maintenance of order and the cause of good government, that frank exposition of general principles and views which appears to be anxiously expected, and which it ought not to be the inclination, and cannot be the interest, of a Minister of this country to withhold.

Gentlemen, the arduous duties in which I am engaged have been imposed upon me through no act of mine. . . . The King, in a crisis of great difficulty, required my services. . . . Was it fit that I should assume that either the object or the effect of the Reform Bill has been to preclude all hope of a successful appeal to the good sense and calm judgement of the people, and so to fetter the prerogative of the Crown, that the King has no free choice among his subjects, but must select his Ministers from one section, and one section only, of public men?

I have taken another course, but I have not taken it without deep and anxious consideration as to the probability that my opinions are so far in unison with those of the constituent body of the United Kingdom as to enable me, and those with whom I am about to act, and whose sentiments are in entire concurrence with my own, to establish such a claim upon public confidence as shall enable us to conduct with vigour and success the Government of this country. . . .

Now I say at once that I will not accept power on the condition of declaring myself an apostate from the principles on which I have heretofore acted. At the same time, I never will admit that I have been, either before or after the Reform Bill, the defender of abuses, or the enemy of judicious reforms. I appeal with confidence, in denial of the charge, to the active part I took in the great question of the Currency – in the consolidation and amendment of the Criminal Law – in the revisal of the whole system of Trial by Jury – to the opinions I have professed, and uniformly acted on, with regard to other branches of the jurisprudence of the country – I appeal to this as a proof that I have not been disposed to acquiesce in acknowledged evils, either from the mere superstitious reverence for ancient usages, or from the dread of labour or responsibility in the application of a remedy. . . .

With respect to the Reform Bill itself, I will repeat now the declaration which I made when I entered the House of Commons as a Member of the Reformed Parliament, that I consider the Reform Bill a final and irrevocable settlement of a great Constitutional question – a settlement which no friend to the peace and welfare of this country would attempt to disturb, either by direct or by insidious means.

Then, as to the spirit of the Reform Bill, and the willingness to adopt and enforce it as a rule of government: if, by adopting the spirit of the Reform Bill, it be meant that we are to live in a perpetual vortex of agitation; that public men can only support themselves in public estimation by adopting every popular impression of the day, – by promising the instant redress of anything which anybody may call an abuse, – by abandoning altogether that great aid of government – more powerful than either law or reason – the respect for ancient rights, and the deference to prescriptive authority; if this be the spirit of the Reform Bill, I will not undertake to adopt it. But if the spirit of the Reform Bill implies merely a careful review of institutions, civil and ecclesiastical, undertaken in a friendly temper, combining, with the firm maintenance of established rights, the correction of proved abuses and the redress of real grievances, – in that case, I can for myself and colleagues undertake to act in such a spirit and with such intentions.

Such declarations of general principle are, I am aware, necessarily vague; but, in order to be more explicit, I will endeavour to apply them practically to some of those questions which have of late attracted the greater share of public interest and attention.

I take first, the inquiry into Municipal Corporations:

It is not my intention to advise the Crown to interrupt the progress of that inquiry, nor to transfer the conduct of it from those to whom it was committed by the late Government. For myself, I gave the best proof that I was not unfriendly to the principle of inquiry, by consenting to be a member of that Committee of the House of Commons on which it was originally devolved. . . .

I will, in the next place, address myself to the questions in which those of our fellow-countrymen who dissent from the doctrines of the Established Church take an especial interest. . . .

In the first place, I supported the measure brought forward by Lord Althorp, the object of which was to exempt all classes from the payment of Church-rates, applying in lieu thereof, out of a branch of the revenue, a certain sum for the building and repair of churches. I never expressed, nor did I entertain, the slightest objection to the principle of a bill of which Lord John Russell was the author, intended to relieve the conscientious scruples of Dissenters in respect to the ceremony of marriage. . . .

I opposed – and I am bound to state that my opinions in that respect have undergone no change – the admission of Dissenters, as a claim of right, into the Universities; but I expressly declared that if regulations, enforced by public authorities superintending the professions of law and medicine, and the studies connected with them, had the effect of conferring advantages of the nature of civil privileges on one class of the King's subjects from which another was excluded – those regulations ought to undergo modification, with the view of placing all the King's subjects, whatever their religious creeds, upon a footing of perfect equality with respect to any civil privilege.

I appeal to the course which I pursued on those several questions, when office must have been out of contemplation; and I ask, with confidence, does that course imply that I was actuated by any illiberal or intolerant spirit towards the Dissenting body, or by an unwillingness to consider fairly the redress of any real grievances?

In the examination of other questions which excited public feeling, I will not omit the Pension List. . . . I voted for the Resolution, moved by Lord Althorp, that pensions on the Civil List ought, for the future, to be confined to such persons only as have just claims to the Royal beneficence, or are entitled to consideration on account either of their personal services to the Crown, or of the performance of duties to the public, or of their scientific or literary eminence. On the Resolution which I thus supported as a private Member of Parliament, I shall scrupulously act as a Minister of the Crown. . . .

Then, as to the great question of Church reform. On that head I have no new professions to make. I cannot give my consent to the alienating of Church property, in any part of the United Kingdom, from strictly Ecclesiastical purposes. But I repeat now the opinions that I have already expressed in Parliament in regard to the Church Establishment in Ireland – that if, by an improved distribution of the revenues of the Church, its just influence can be extended, and the true interests of the Established religion promoted, all other considerations should be made subordinate to the advancement of objects of such paramount importance. . . .

With regard to alterations in the laws which govern our Ecclesiastical Establishment, I have had no recent opportunity of giving that grave consideration to a subject of the deepest interest, which could alone justify me in making any public declaration of opinion. It is a subject which must undergo the fullest deliberation, and into that deliberation the Government will enter, with the sincerest desire to remove every abuse that can impair the efficiency of the Establishment, to extend the sphere of its usefulness, and to strengthen and confirm its just claims upon the respect and affections of the people.

It is unnecessary for my purpose to enter into further details. I have said enough, with respect to general principles and their practical application to public measures, to indicate the spirit in which the King's Government is prepared to act. Our object will be – the maintenance of peace – the scrupulous and honourable fulfilment, without reference to their original policy, of all existing engagements with Foreign Powers, – the support of public credit – the enforcement of strict economy – and the just and impartial consideration of what is due to all interests – agricultural, manufacturing, and commercial.

. . . with a resolution to persevere, which nothing could inspire but the strong impulse of public duty, the consciousness of upright motives, and the firm belief that the people of this country will so far maintain the prerogative of the King, as to give to the Ministers of his choice, not an implicit confidence, but a fair trial.

I am, Gentlemen,
With affectionate regard,
Most faithfully yours,
ROBERT PEEL

Peel *Memoirs*, ii.58-67

4 The Conservative Party in the 1830s: A Contemporary View

The extract below gives a description by a sympathetic writer of what Tamworth Conservatism meant to its adherents in the years between Peel's 1834-5 administration and the electoral triumph of 1841. The author, Sir John Benn Walsh, Bt., (1798-1881), politician and pamphleteer, of Warfield Park, Berks, was educated at Eton and Christ Church, Oxford, High Sheriff of Berkshire 1823 and Radnorshire 1825; Conservative M.P. for Sudbury 1830-4, 1838-40, and for Radnorshire 1840-68; and Lord Lieutenant of Radnorshire 1842-75.

(1836)

I have sometimes heard it asked, What is a Conservative – what does the word mean? I think that I can give a short and clear definition. A Conservative is a man attached upon principle to the English Constitution, to the Established Church, to our mixed institutions. Well, but so is, or at least so was, a Whig of the old school. There is another characteristic – a Conservative is one who, having this loyalty to the Constitution, believes it is threatened with subversion by the encroachments of democracy, and is prepared to defend it against that danger. The Conservative party, therefore, includes all those shades and degrees of political opinion, from the disciple of moderate Whig principles to the most devoted champion of ancient usages, who agree in these two points – attachment to King, Lords, Commons, Church, and State, and a belief that there is a pressing danger of these institutions being overborne by the weight of the Democracy.

. . . I trust that the preceding remarks may convey to my readers juster ideas of the composition, principles, and objects of the Conservative party, than they would derive from the polemical articles of the ministerial journals. They consist in these positions: – That the

Conservative party is not identical with the Tory party, – that it includes, indeed, the Tories, but that it is a more comprehensive term, and that the basis is a wider one; – that the Conservative party may be defined to consist of all that part of the community who are attached to the Constitution in Church and State, and who believe that it is threatened with subversion by the encroachments of democracy. That this definition does not necessarily suppose an abstract horror of all innovation, or an illiberal and contracted view of politics. That, on the contrary, the opinions and feelings of the great body of the Conservatives in this country are liberal, candid, and generous. That they do not oppose a dogged resistance to the progress of improvement, but that they are prepared to proceed upon the conviction, that they gain many steps in advance by adopting much that has already been accomplished. They consider that the march of democracy, with its eternal warfare against all that exists, is a retrograde one.

With regard to its numbers, and social position, the Conservative party does not consist alone of the Peerage, – of what are invidiously called the 'privileged orders', or of the political adherents of former ministries, – it embraces a vast proportion of the numerical amount of the population. It extends into every quarter of the empire, and every class of the community. It rests upon the support of the majority of the property of the country, and it is sustained by the attachment to the National Church.

I do not wish to underrate all the formidable influences opposed to it; the radical and democratic spirit prevalent in the large town constituencies in England, and still more in Scotland; the hostility of the Dissenters; the power of Mr O'Connell in Ireland, and the organized opposition of the Roman Catholic population. Admitting, as I fully do, that we are in the unfortunate condition of a nation divided upon questions of vital importance into great opposing parties, and distracted by all the bitter animosities, which the keenest party strife can occasion; I yet claim for the Conservatives the rank of a national party, comprising a vast section of the people.

Sir J. B. Walsh, *Chapters of Contemporary History* (1836), pp. 77-8, 87-9

5   Parties and Politics: A Whig View

In the general election of 1837 Lord John Russell and his Whig colleague, G. Poulett Scrope, standing for re-election in the west-country clothing town of Stroud, were returned with large majorities over a Conservative candidate. On 23 July, at a banquet given to celebrate the victory, Russell made a speech which soon became famous. It was later reprinted and issued as a pamphlet, and attacked by J. W. Croker in the Tory *Quarterly Review*. The following extracts from the speech as reported in *The Times* differ slightly from the subsequent edited version. *(July 1835)*   *Russell*

Lord J. Russell, in returning thanks on the part of himself and his colleagues, said, that as there were many present from different parts of the country who had not attended the nomination, he thought this now a fit time to state what had been the acts of the present Administration, and of that under Earl Grey. [He prefaced his remarks with an attack on the fifty years of 'Tory administration' from the time of the younger Pitt and a description of the state of the country on the death of George IV in 1830.] When the Tories left the country in such a state, it was no wonder that they now wished to give up the name of 'Tory', and to assume some title which would not be so much associated with their former acts. (Cheers) Yet now the country was called upon to pay to the successors of those Tories all possible respect under their newly assumed name of Conservatives (cheers and laughter), which, after all, was only an alias for the name of Tory. (Cheers) They were, however, entitled to the name of Conservatives on this ground – that they were Conservative of all abuses. If they chose to abolish the old name of Tory and Whig, he had no objection to be distinguished from the new name of Conservative, and to be called a Reformer. (Cheers) The Reformers had the testimony of history in their favour. Luther was a Reformer; Leo X., who opposed him, was a Conservative; Galileo, who had made so many important discoveries in science, was a Reformer; the Inquisition, who persecuted him, was Conservative. (Cheers) The early Christians who had willingly laid down their lives in that sacred cause were Reformers; Nero, who put so many of them to torture and to death, was a Conservative. (Cheers) If then they wished to change old names into new, he was ready to be called a Reformer (cheers), as one not wishing to be known as a Conservative, but as one wishing to see the progress of improvement – to see the country advance in all that was good, and generous, and enlightened. (Cheers) He was unwilling to see the country go back or stand still in her great institutions. He was an advocate for reform in the truest sense of the word, and he would do all in his power to promote those measures of reform of which he was the avowed advocate. If other measures of reform were proposed, he was ready to discuss them, and if they could be shown to be good, in God's name let them have them (cheers); but let them not be deterred by any bugbear from boldly and fearlessly arguing them in the first instance, and if right from adopting them. (Cheers) The noble lord then took a review of the leading acts of the governments of Lord Grey and Viscount Melbourne, and observed, that when they considered the subjects of reform of the criminal law, the abolition of slavery, and the Municipal Corporation Act, they would believe that these Governments had not been idle in their respective periods of power. (Cheers) In the opening of the China trade, the weight of the East India Company was opposed to them. In putting an end to slavery, they had the opposition of all the West India interest. In all great reforms they had to oppose some powerful body. In the municipal corporations they had to oppose many large bodies. In the church reforms they were opposed by the deans and chapters. (Cheers) They were also in other reforms opposed by the prejudices of large portions of the people. For instance, in the amendment of the poor laws, the Government had to encounter the great opposition of large bodies of the poor, who had been supported in idleness at the expense of the hard-working and industrious. To such an extent had this gone, that in one county in which a near relation of his resided, the farmers had to sit up in turn to protect their property from the acts of the incendiary. Such was the extent of that evil, that the Minister of that day, while he admitted it, also declared that he had not the means of meeting it. A reform Government alone had had the courage to grapple with the evil, and to place the poor laws on that footing which would tend to promote the comfort of the really industrious classes. Speaking of Ireland, the noble lord said that it was not a question of supporting Catholic or Protestant, but they rather went on the Protestant principle of leaving matters open to discussion, for the present Ministry went upon the true Protestant principle of not subjecting any man to persecution on account of his religious opinions. The Ministers would bring in such measures as they thought right, leaving it to the country to pronounce an opinion upon those subjects. As to other topics – the duration of Parliament, vote by ballot, and universal suffrage, he would say, that when the Reform Act was proposed he had proposed to disfranchise 50 of the smaller boroughs, and to deprive 50 of the next smaller of one member. It was proposed to limit Parliaments to five years, and if the ballot were to be used, and Parliaments shortened, it was proposed that the right of voting should be raised from 10l. to 20l., but the 10l. franchise was at length adopted without any change in the duration of Parliaments. The bill was passed, and though there were parts of it which were open for discussion, still he must say that

the less frequently such a measure as the Reform Act was discussed the
better, and the more stable the law would become. . . . After noticing
the great additions that had from time to time been made to the
House of Lords of persons of the same political party, and the effects
which had resulted from it, the noble lord went on to observe, that
he was sure that whenever the opinions of the people were unequi-
vocally declared, the Lords would know their station, and would
not oppose the wishes of the country. At all events, he was not for
making a change in the great institutions of the country. Let those who
would try the experiment take its consequences; he would never be a
party to it, for he was sure the prosperity of the country depended on
the due maintenance of all its institutions in that state in which they
had been recognized by the constitution. . . . The country had flourished
in the greatest prosperity, under the reigns of female sovereigns. He
hoped that the present reign would be also distinguished, but in a
higher degree. The reigns of Elizabeth and of Anne had been distinguished for great victories over foreign foes. He hoped that the
present reign would have all the vigour and all the prosperity of that of
Elizabeth without its tyranny, and of that of Anne without the necessity
of its foreign battles.

The Times, 31 July 1837

6   Whigs and Liberals, 1838

The general election of 1837, made necessary by the accession of Queen
Victoria, was the hardest-fought between the first and second reform acts. It
resulted in further losses to the government, especially in the English counties;
and their majority was reduced to about thirty. A feature of the election was
the defeat of several well-known Radicals – Hume in Middlesex, Roebuck at
Bath, Ewart at Liverpool, Col. Thompson at Maidstone, and Hutt at Hull. On
the government side of the House the central moderate elements had been
strengthened at the expense of both conservative Whigs and extreme Radicals.
This emergence of a more united Liberal party was reflected in various shifts
of cabinet policy between 1838 and 1841, notably allowing the ballot to be
open question (i.e. one for which government supporters were allowed to vote)
and accepting the need for a revision of the Corn Laws. The *Westminster Review*
founded by Jeremy Bentham and James Mill in 1824 as the organ of the philo-
sophic utilitarians, represented a sophisticated intellectual radical viewpoint
in politics.

The result of the late elections enables us in like manner to say, England
is moderate-Radical. Of the different shades of opinion composing the

majority (those who are returned under Tory colours we do [not] speak of) the Whigs are considerably reduced in strength, and we have lost a few of the more decided Radicals; among whom it will be discreditable to the nation if Mr Roebuck at least does not immediately find another seat. But the moderate Radicals have even increased in numbers. Several adherents of the Ministry have made a move towards Radicalism, and of the new Liberal members (very numerous in this Parliament), the moderate Radicals form a large proportion. Such persons compose the great majority of the Reform party in the higher and middle classes. They consist chiefly of men who have not till lately been active politicians, or whose opinions have advanced with events. They have hitherto not approved, or not responded to, any attacks on the Ministers; and, in all their movements, they are anxious to carry the Ministers with them. They are decidedly for King, Lords, and Commons. They have generally not yet made up their minds to the necessity of any organic change in the House of Lords. They are not for Universal Suffrage. Many of them are for the Church; not such as the Tories have made it, but yet the Church, such a Church in reality as we already have in pretence; far less radically altered in its constitution than *we* deem necessary, both for religion and for good government. But these men, so little inclined to extreme opinions, are universally for the Ballot. They are for shortening the duration of Parliaments. They are for abridging the expenses of elections; simplifying the qualifications of voters; abolishing the rate-paying clauses. They are for abolishing, or consolidating into districts like those of Wales and Scotland, the small borough constituencies. They are for abrogating the Corn-Laws. Friends as many of them are to the principle of a Church Establishment conformable to what they conceive to be the theory of the Church of England, they recognize none of the conditions which render such an institution legitimate in the monstrous anomaly calling itself the Irish Church; a Church forced upon a conquered people by a handful of foreigners, who confiscated their land, and for ages hunted them down like beasts of prey.

We affirm, and if the Ministers do not know it the first few divisions will teach it them, that these are the opinions generally prevailing among the new liberal English members. These men represent the average strength of the Reform spirit; those who go further being in number and weight a full set-off against those who do not go so far. . . . Let Ministers remember, that no party ever for long together recognized its hindmost men as its chiefs: the leaders are always either those who precede the rest in making up their minds and pointing out the course to be followed, or those who can at least be counted upon for adopting and giving effect to the opinion of the majority.

The Ballot is necessary to their continuance in power; it is demanded by the almost unanimous opinion of their supporters; and the country is now aware that they themselves have no rooted aversion to it, no objection but such as these considerations ought to remove. We have hitherto regarded Lord John Russell as its chief opponent. We should never think of addressing a man of Lord John Russell's character with any argument appealing solely to his interest; but from the revelations in his speech at Stroud (which have raised him in the opinion of all reasonable men much more than his previous opposition to the Ballot had lowered him) we now know that his objection was never one of principle.... Why, then, has he since opposed it? For a reason not necessarily disparaging to him: he thought that a statesman, who has to consider not only his own conviction, but the rules according to which *masses* of men may most wisely regulate their collective conduct, should give a fair trial to one great change, and allow its full effects to unfold themselves before beginning another. To this we cannot object: but what is to be considered a fair trial? The majority for the Reformers has dwindled from three hundred to twenty-six, and at last to twelve: is it necessary to the sufficiency of the trial, that this last remnant should disappear?

... You *have* the power; you have it perhaps for the first time; certainly for the last. You have it, if what your adherents say be true – if you hold the option of dissolving the Parliament. With the knowledge that you have that power, together with that of creating Peers, you might perhaps carry the question even in this Parliament. But if it fail, throw yourself once more upon the electors.

Westminster Review, xxviii.8-10 (1838)

7   A Disillusioned Whig, 1838

The election of 1837 confirmed many liberals in their view that the full benefit of reform could not be realised without further improvements in electoral machinery, especially the introduction of the ballot, an extension of the suffrage, and triennial parliaments. This brought up the question whether the Reform Act of 1832 was regarded by its authors as a final measure or not. The reluctance of Lord Melbourne to sanction any move towards the ballot led to Russell's 'finality' speech in the House of Commons at the start of the new session in November 1837 which brought him much unpopularity and the nickname of 'Finality Jack'. His argument on that occasion that a further instalment of reform would be a breach of faith with those who had supported the bill in 1832 as a permanent and satisfactory settlement, was one that was felt strongly by the 'old Whigs' though they did not all trust the government to resist much longer the demand for the ballot. Sir James Graham, a former Whig and one of the Committee of Four which drafted the reform bill, had resigned from the government with Stanley in 1834 and by 1838 was closely identified with the Conservative opposition. His correspondent was Lord John Russell's elder brother.

Sir James Graham to Lord Tavistock   29 August 1838

Already, in my opinion – I had also believed, in the opinion of the Government of Lord Grey – 'in recasting the representative system that point has been reached beyond which it is impossible to proceed with safety', if the rights of property are to be respected, and an aristocracy maintained.

The struggle against the progressive advance of democracy may be more or less protracted, and may end in unforeseen results. But my part was taken at the passing of the Reform Act. I pledged myself to resist the Ballot, short Parliaments, and further extension of the Suffrage, in consideration of the great change which we were then enabled peaceably to effect. Reason, honour, duty, combine to restrain me from assenting directly or indirectly to any of those measures on which the Radicals insist, and which inevitably tend to the destruction of our mixed form of Government. The resistance may be hopeless, but I am bound to make it; and it would not be so desperate, if all who promised to resist were united, and in time opposed a manly front to the open designs of that Radical party which is now stronger in the House of Commons than the Whigs.

If Ballot be made an open question, it will be carried. This mode of treating measures which affect the foundations of our policy weakens every day the main-spring of government itself, and practically gives an advantage to the more violent members of a Cabinet over their more prudent colleagues.

C. S. Parker, *Sir James Graham* (1907), i.268

8 Peel on the Position of Prime Minister, 1841

Having been beaten on a vote of no confidence in June 1841 the government dissolved parliament. The general election which followed produced a majority of about eighty for the Conservatives. The new parliament met in August and

following a defeat by ninety-one votes on the Address, Melbourne's ministry
resigned office. After a short adjournment while Peel formed his new ministry,
parliament reassembled on 16 September. The speech from which the extract
is taken was made by Peel in a debate on 17 September on going into committee
of supply. He was replying to charges by Lord John Russell that the composition of his party and ministry would prevent him from following an enlightened
policy in economic affairs, especially in connection with the Corn Laws.
Similar charges had been made about Peel's future policy towards Ireland in the
debate on the Address in August and had been rejected by Peel in terms similar
to those used below.

The noble lord, after having, not reluctantly, but at once, admitted,
that I have triumphed over the difficulties which threatened my course
with respect to Ireland, says, that on account of the composition of the
government, and the menaces which have been held out in parliament,
it will be impossible for me to perform my public duty on other questions
which concern the domestic policy of the empire. I can assure the noble
lord that it is my intention to act upon a sense of public duty, and to
propose those measure to parliament which my own conviction of
public duty shall lead me to think desirable. Sir, it is right that there
should be a distinct understanding as to the terms on which a public
man holds office. The force of circumstances, and a sense of duty to the
country, have compelled me to undertake the harassing and laborious
task, in the performance of which I now stand before you. What can
be my inducement to undertake that task, and to make the sacrifices
which it entails? – what but the hope of rendering service to my
country, and of acquiring an honourable fame? Is it credible that I
would go through the labours which are daily imposed upon me, if I
did not claim for myself the liberty of proposing to parliament those
measures which I shall believe conducive to the public welfare? I will
claim that liberty. I will propose those measures: and I do with
confidence assure this House, that no consideration of mere political
support shall induce me to alter them. I will not hold office by the
servile tenure which would compel me to be the instrument of carrying
other men's opinions into effect. I do not estimate lightly the distinctions which office confers. To any man who is fit to hold it, its only
value must be, not the patronage which the possessor is enabled to
confer, nor the personal distinction it confers on him, but the opportunity which is afforded to him of doing good to his country. And the
moment I shall be convinced that that power is denied me, to be exercised in accordance with my own views of duty, I tell every one who
hears me, that he confers on me no personal obligation in having

placed me in this office. Free as the winds, I shall reserve to myself the power of retiring from the discharge of its onerous and harassing functions, the moment I feel that I cannot discharge them with satisfaction to the public and the approval of my own conscience.

Peel *Speeches*, iii.810-11

9 Clarendon's Memorandum on the State of the Whig Party, June, 1846

The Liberal opposition 1841-6 had not been very united or effective and Lord John Russell had failed to take the opportunity offered in December 1845 to rehabilitate the Whigs and gain popularity by repealing the Corn Laws. He took office six months later as a result of the defeat of Peel's government on the Irish coercion bill by a combination of liberals, Irish, and a section (less than a third) of the protectionist Conservatives who had voted against the repeal of the Corn Laws. The general election of 1847 produced a much-divided House of Commons in which the nominal government party was roughly equal to Peelites and Protectionists combined. The general body of liberals was however less united than in the 1835-41 period partly because of the independent Radicals under Cobden and Hume, partly because of the quarrel between Dissenters and the government over education (see above III, 9). The memorandum quoted below was written for circulation among the newly-formed Whig cabinet following discussions on 29 June over ways of recruiting fresh political strength. The writer, Lord Clarendon, one of the few supporters of the admission of Cobden to the cabinet, was an intelligent, liberal, strong-minded aristocrat who had just been appointed president of the Board of Trade. Originally a diplomat and administrator, he had been Lord Privy Seal in Melbourne's cabinet 1839-41, was Lord Lieutenant of Ireland 1847-52, and later served as Foreign Secretary under Aberdeen, Palmerston, Russell and Gladstone.

There is nothing which more requires the true conservative process of reform than the Whig party. For years past its vitality and vigor have been fading; the roots it formerly struck into the country have withered; it no longer derives strength from public sympathy. It is considered to be aristocratical in its opinions, exclusive in its personnel, and guided by past historical reminiscences rather than by present public opinion. As a political party it is thought to be nearly effete, and, as the means of governing, a matter of history rather than of fact. Its reconstruction upon a far broader basis is now indispensable, and though the present moment is one of singular difficulty, yet on the other hand it does afford great means for forming a powerful administration. With tact, decision and promptness the scattered fragments of parties now floating about might be collected together and united; out of present chaos might spring something at least approaching to that order and harmony which all reasonable men now desire.

A fusion, so far as practicable with some of the Peelite party and some of the extreme Free-traders, would be a symptom that the Whig party recognised that their present position was owing to accident, and not to any general wish of the country to see them in power. This would at once excite the sympathy and call forth the support of those sections of the community best able to confer strength upon a government under the present peculiar circumstances – in fact, to constitute a government fairly representing the industrial mind and conservative progress of the country. Nothing should be done to offend or alarm the aristocracy or the landed interest, but all attempts to conciliate them or to render them reliable supporters of Lord John Russell's government will fail, unless a stand-still, if not a retrograde policy be adopted, which must inevitably estrange that class of persons and opinions upon which all future governments must depend. The country will not stand still; an impetus had been given to men's minds that cannot be checked: wants and hopes have been excited that must be satisfied; commercial, financial and social reforms have been commenced and must be continued. The aristocracy – the party that has already announced its intention to promote a backward agitation, and hopes in two years to acquire strength sufficient to govern the country upon the principle of undoing all that has been done with much difficulty and sacrifice – cannot lend itself to the labors which a Liberal government has on hand. . . . No voluntary aid from the Protectionists should be rejected, but none should be courted by any futile attempt at shaping the policy of the government to meet their objects. They now profess to be disinterested: they ask nothing for themselves: they pretend a desire to repair the injustice of 1841 and a readiness to support the only government now possible under existing circumstances. They are not sincere: with ulterior views such as they entertain, they cannot honestly or with reference to their own interests support the policy which it is the duty of Lord John Russell to pursue. They already have indicated their wishes: they have expressed a hope that Mr Cobden may not form part of the government, for they know the irreparable mischief which his exclusion would do Lord J. R. in the towns and among the classes where we must naturally look for support. They know that this would produce lukewarmness and subsequent secession on the part of many Liberals, which would leave the Protectionists masters of the field, able to dictate their own terms to Lord J. R., who must either succumb to them, or, through his own weakness, relinquish the task he has undertaken. They think they would then be the only indispensable party, because the only one possessing strength enough to form an administration; but in this they would be deceived, for all this time Sir R. Peel would not be idle or unobservant of the trap set for Lord J. R. He has not broken up his party and embarked on a *middle-class* policy without being prepared to carry it out to its full results, altho' he may do so in his own peculiar and furtive way. If he perceives any retrograde or stand-still symptoms in Lord J. R. he will outbid him a little as he has already been much outbidden by Lord J. R.; but that little will always be sufficient to rally round him the free-traders, manufacturers and middle classes, who are already better disposed to him than to Lord J. R., because they think him more squeezable and more likely to carry out the system of direct taxation which they are bent upon establishing. The composition of the Cabinet is therefore of the utmost importance as indicative of its policy. Should the names of its members not satisfy public expectation, and should its acts fall short of public requirements, the dissolution of Parliament will create a new and independent Peelite party, which will be held to represent national progress and bid fair to extinguish the Whigs, as a party, for ever.

Sir H. Maxwell, *Life and Letters of Fourth Earl of Clarendon* (1913), i.265-7

V

CHARTISM

1 The People's Charter

The London Working Men's Association was founded in 1836 by an elite group of London artisans and trade-unionists to promote the social and intellectual progress of the working classes. William Lovett, a cabinet-maker, was secretary and Henry Hetherington, a printer and publisher, was treasurer. In 1837 the Association drew up a petition to parliament in favour of radical electoral reform which was the basis of the subsequent Charter. The petition roused the interest of the more radical M.P.s and following a conference between the two groups in the summer of 1837 it was agreed to redraft the petition as a parliamentary bill. A joint committee was appointed for this purpose consisting of six M.P.s (D. O'Connell, J. A. Roebuck, J. T. Leader, C. Hindley, Col. Thompson and S. Crawford) and six members of the Association (Lovett, Hetherington, J. Watson, J. Cleave, H. Vincent, and R. Moore). The committee took no immediate action, however, and in the end the bill was drawn up by Lovett and Francis Place, who had taken a strong interest in the Association since its foundation. The draft was considered by the committee of twelve and a preamble added by Roebuck. It was then published as the People's Charter in May 1838. Three times presented to the House of Commons, by Attwood in 1839, by Duncombe in 1842, and by Feargus O'Connor in 1848, it failed to attract more than derisory support in the legislature.

THE PEOPLE'S CHARTER

Being the Outline of an Act to provide for the just Representation of the People of Great Britain and Ireland in the Commons' House of Parliament: embracing the Principles of Universal Suffrage, no Property Qualification, Annual Parliaments, Equal Representation, Payment of Members, and Vote by Ballot.

Prepared by a Committee of twelve persons, six Members of Parliament and six Members of the London Working Men's Association, and addressed to the People of the United Kingdom.

An Act to provide for the just Representation of the People of Great Britain and Ireland, in the Commons' House of Parliament. Whereas to insure, in as far as it is best possible by human forethought and wisdom, the just government of the people, it is necessary to subject those who have the power of making the laws, to a wholesome and strict responsibility to those whose duty it is to obey them when made:

And, whereas, this responsibility is best enforced through the instrumentality of a body which emanates directly from, and is itself immediately subject to, the whole people, and which completely represents their feelings and their interests:

And, whereas, as the Commons' House of Parliament now exercises in the name and on the supposed behalf of the people, the power of making the laws, it ought, in order to fulfil with wisdom and with honesty the great duties imposed on it, to be made the faithful and accurate representation of the people's wishes, feelings and interests.

Be it therefore Enacted,

That from and after the passing of this Act, every male inhabitant of these realms be entitled to vote for the election of a Member of Parliament, subject however to the following conditions.

1. That he be a native of these realms, or a foreigner who has lived in this country upwards of two years, and been naturalized.

2. That he be twenty-one years of age.

3. That he be not proved insane when the list of voters are revised.

4. That he be not convicted of felony within six months from and after the passing of this Act.

5. That his electoral rights be not suspended for bribery at elections, or for personation, or for forgery of election certificates, according to the penalties of this Act. . . .

ELECTORAL DISTRICTS

I. Be it enacted, that for the purpose of obtaining an equal representation of the people in the Commons' House of Parliament, the United Kingdom be divided into 300 electoral districts.

II. That each such district contain, as nearly as may be, an equal number of inhabitants.

III. That the number of inhabitants be taken from the last census, and as soon as possible after the next ensuing decennial census shall have been taken, the electoral districts be made to conform thereto.

IV. That each electoral district be named after the principal city or borough within its limits.

V. That each electoral district return one representative to sit in the Commons' House of Parliament, and no more. . . .

Returning Officer, and his Duties

I-III. [Returning officers to be elected for each electoral district every three years.]

ARRANGEMENT FOR NOMINATIONS

I. Be it enacted, that for the purpose of guarding against too great a number of candidates, who might otherwise be heedlessly proposed, as well as for giving time for the electors to enquire into the merits of the persons who may be nominated for Members of Parliament, as well as for returning officers, that all nominations be taken as hereinafter directed.

II. That for all general elections of Members of Parliament, a requisition of the following form, signed by at least one hundred qualified electors of the district, be delivered to the returning officer of the district between the 1st and the 10th day of May in each year; and that such requisition constitute the nomination of such person as a candidate for the district. . . .

XI. That no other qualification shall be required for members to serve in the Commons' House of Parliament, than the choice of the electors. . . .

ARRANGEMENT FOR ELECTIONS

I-VI. [Election of M.P.s to take place annually in June; electors to vote only in the district in which they are registered; voting to be by secret ballot.]

DURATION OF PARLIAMENT

I. Be it enacted, that the Members of the House of Commons chosen as aforesaid, shall meet on the first Monday in June in each year, and continue their sittings from time to time as they may deem it convenient, till the first Monday in June the following, when the next new Parliament is to be chosen: they shall be eligible to be re-elected.

II. That during an adjournment, they be liable to be called together by the executive, in cases of emergency.

III. That a register be kept of the daily attendance of each member, which at the close of the session shall be printed as a sessional paper, showing how the members have attended. . . .

PAYMENT OF MEMBERS

I. Be it enacted, that every Member of the House of Commons be entitled, at the close of the session, to a writ of expenses on the Treasury, for his legislative duties in the public service, and shall be paid £500 per annum.

The Chartist Circular, 5 Oct. 1839

2   The People's Charter: An Explanatory Dialogue

The continuous intellectual history of Chartism goes back to the eighteenth century. The main ideas of the Charter were anticipated in Major Cartwright's plan of parliamentary reform in 1776 which in turn provided the basis for the programme of the working-class London Corresponding Society of 1791-8 of which Francis Place had been a member. All six points of the Charter are to be found in a nine-point programme issued by the Westminster reform committee of 1780; they are succinctly conveyed in the Benthamite formula of 'Secrecy, Universality, Equality and Annuality of Suffrage'. The Chartists were therefore merely repeating a political philosophy which had been made familiar by radical books, pamphlets and speeches for two generations. The dialogue printed below elucidates for a popular audience the reasons and arguments behind the Chartist demands.

To those who have but a partial knowledge of the political principles for which we contend, the following simple elucidation of the Charter merits an attentive perusal. It is extracted from an ably-conducted journal, that for many years past has been the principal organ of the Whigs in our sister kingdom.[1] . . . 'Good morning to you, friend: I understand you profess Chartist principles, and as I confess, in common with many others, my ignorance of what Chartism means, I should be obliged by your informing me what is the meaning of the term 'Chartist'? It is one who is an advocate for the People's Charter.

The People's Charter! pray, what is that? It is the outline of an Act of Parliament, drawn up by a Committee of the London Working Men's Association, and six Members of Parliament; and embraces the six cardinal points of Radical Reform.

What are these principles? There are six, and they are named as follows: – *Universal Suffrage, Annual Parliaments, Vote by Ballot, Equal Representation, Payment of Members, No Property Qualification.*

[1] *The Northern Whig*, Belfast.

Do you mean by Universal Suffrage, that men, women, and children should vote? No, we do not; it is often difficult to find a term which shall clearly express what you mean, and, perhaps, Universal Adult Male Suffrage would have been a more near approach to our meaning; but we mean by the term, that every man twenty-one years of age, unconvicted of crime, and of sound mind, should have a vote in the election of the Representatives who are to make the laws he is called upon to obey, and who lay on the taxes he is required to pay.

Do you think this essential to obtain and secure good government? I do, for the following reasons: – First, because the possession of the franchise is the only difference between a freeman and the Russian serf, who is sold with the land and the cattle, as part of the farm stock; or the slave of South Carolina, where it is punishable to teach a slave to read: it is the only security against bad laws, and for good government, which otherwise depend on the caprice or fears of the master-class, who make laws; and, while the exclusive few have a profitable interest in bad laws, there will be no barrier to tyranny and corruption, but the fear of resistance on the part of the enslaved many.

Why do you prefer Annual Parliaments to Septennial, as at present? Because we should be enabled, by this means, to get rid of a bad servant, at the end of one year, instead of being fixed with him for seven, as at present.

But would a man be able, in one year, to obtain an insight into the forms of Parliament, and would it be prudent to dismiss a man as soon as he became useful? This is begging the question; we should not dismiss an honest and capable man, and the sooner a dishonest or incapable one is dismissed, the better. With respect to obtaining an acquaintance with the forms of Parliament, every man must, at his first entrance, be ignorant of the practice of the House: and the knowledge he would acquire, in the first year, would enhance his value, and, provided he was honest and capable, would ensure his re-election.

By Voting by Ballot, of course you mean secret voting: what benefit is expected from that? The prevention of bribery or intimidation at elections; or the influencing a man to vote against his own will or judgment.

Oh! but consider how un-English it is in character, and what lying and deception it will occasion? I am not so bigoted an admirer of English customs as to refuse to adopt the regulations of other countries, where they are proved to be beneficial; besides, the practice is not so un-English as you seem to think; those very consistent and independent gentlemen who profess so much care for the morals of the electors, and such a horror of the Ballot, constantly make use of it for the protection of themselves, in the election of the members in their Clubs. With regard to the deception, it is admitted that the Ballot is merely a remedy for a disease; and, if it can be proved (which I believe it can, to demonstration) that the evil the Ballot will remove is so enormous, compared with any it can possibly inflict, the question will resolve itself into a balance of evils, and, of course, the lesser evil is preferable to the greater.

Pray what is meant by Equal Representation? It means that the country should be divided into equal electoral districts (say 300) each containing, as near as conveniently may be, an equal number of inhabitants, and each district to send one Representative to Parliament.

Is it not divided into electoral districts at present? It is, but not equal; for instance: – Harwich sends two Members to Parliament, and numbers 156 electors, while Westminster, with 13,268 electors, sends no more; so that, if it is right that Harwich should send two Members, Westminster should send 170. Nor is this a solitary instance. There are ten Boroughs sending twenty Members, the total amount of whose electors amount to 2,411, while ten other Boroughs also sending Members, number 86,072 electors; so, if it be right that the ten small Boroughs send twenty Members, the ten large Boroughs should send about 700!!

What proportion do the electors bear to the whole male population, above twenty-one years? About one to seven and a half; the total number of registered electors being 838,519; and the number of males above 21 years is 6,023,752.

We will now come, if you please, to the next point of your Charter, which, I think, is Payment of Members; do you not think, if men capable of the duty can be found to execute it for nothing, it would save money? I doubt much whether it would save money. If I give a servant no wages, and he paid for his place, as servants in hotels and Members of Parliament do at present, I should suppose he expected to make more by it than he could fairly ask as wages.

But it seems to be a sort of degradation, that a Member of Parliament should receive wages like a servant. You have no good grounds to think so. Does any one consider the great Officers of State, the Judges, &c. &c. degraded by receiving the salaries they do? If a man devotes his time and talents, he is fairly entitled to remuneration; and it is proposed by the Charter to give each Member £500 per annum. Besides, there is nothing new in this: Members of Parliament used to receive wages. There is an account, in an ancient chronicle, of a Member of Parliament, who was also Recorder of the Borough, who agreed, upon condition of being re-elected, to forego his wages. We may imagine, like the Modern Members, he discovered there were pickings in Parliament, which would enable him to work for nothing, and pay for his place.

The last is No Property Qualification. – Pray what is meant by that? We mean that the choice of the electors shall be the only qualification necessary.

But, would you send men to Parliament not worth a shilling? I doubt whether a man without a shilling would be elected; but the present property qualification is a farce; if a man has money or interest enough to get into Parliament, he can purchase a sham qualification for £100. But why should not a poor man, if he has ability sufficient, and a majority of the electors have confidence in him, be elected? If none but rich men are sent to Parliament, the feelings of the poor cannot be fairly represented. In Norway, the peasant farmer, in his grey home-spun doublet, sits, in the House of Deputies, beside the noble; and there the laws are just and equal, while here, because the law-makers are the few, the laws are unequal and oppressive.

But where is the clause for the distribution of property? Have you forgotten that? That is a base and slanderous calumny, which those who profit by things as they are, have forged, to damage our cause. There never was the slightest foundation for such a charge, although judges on the bench, and parsons on the pulpit, have not scrupled to give currency to the falsehood.

What are the benefits you anticipate from the adoption of the Charter? The repeal of bad laws, and the making of good laws in their stead; a reduction of taxation, by which the productive industry of the nation would be increased; the abolition of the enormous abuses of the civil and criminal law, which amount, in most cases, to an utter denial of justice to the poor; a large and liberal system of National Education, without reference to creed, which would tend at once to diminish crime, by striking at its root; the cost of the civil and criminal justice, in this country, is above two millions, while only £30,000 is devoted to National Education. Would it not be far better to diminish the former amount by increasing the latter?

Why, this certainly appears reasonable: are there any other benefits you expect? Yes, certainly; more than I can now enumerate: there is the expense of the State, the civil list, as it is called, amounting to about £1,000,000 sterling, while the United States civil list is not £20,000: I think we might be as well, or better governed for less money, by half, than we pay at present.

Oh! but consider the expenditure of this money makes good for trade – what should we do without it? That is a mistaken notion; if the money were left in the pockets of the people, they would spend it in comforts for themselves, and thereby make as good for trade as if it was spent in luxury, by idle and useless placemen.

Mr Doubtful – Well, your objects seem more reasonable than I expected, so I wish you success. Good morning to you.

The Chartist Circular, 2 Jan. 1841

3   The Roots of Violence

By 1840 Chartism had outgrown its origins and become a wide and complex movement under various leaders and fed by unemployment, poverty and social discontent. Among the early grievances which contributed to its rapid growth was the new Poor Law (see below **IX, 2**) which from 1836-7 was beginning to be introduced into the northern industrial areas. By many Chartists it was regarded as a direct and sinister consequence of the middle-class victory of 1832. Major-General Sir Charles James Napier was in command of the northern district (1839-41) during the first outbreak of violent Chartism which accompanied the economic slump, unemployment and high prices of the years 1837-42. He was a warm-hearted practical soldier with strong social sympathies and little patience with politicians of either party. The letter which follows was written to his brother William, the historian of the Peninsular War.

[To Colonel W. Napier] January 19th. [1840] – Misery is running riot through the greatest part of this district, that is to say through the manufacturing parts; the agricultural parts suffer less perhaps, at all events being less condensed it is less perceptible. At Nottingham the gentry are really very good-natured: the mayor and one or two more got up a meeting, and in a few days near £4000 was subscribed, despite of the exertions of the poor law people, who said we were encouraging idleness. The poor here have resolved to die rather than go into the union houses, and I have not the least doubt that numbers would have starved sooner than go there; certainly they would have resisted hunger until the feebler bodies of their children perished, or been so reduced as never to recover their health. Many who were willing were refused admittance. . . . However the misery is so horrid, the poor law rules are necessarily broken and put aside, and relief out of door is given perforce. We have 800 men paid by the private subscription; and, horror of horrors! 200 of them rank Chartists, employed by the mayor's order, at which some people here cannot sleep in their beds: they would ere this have slept less if they had a 'vigorous mayor', for the town would have been burned. My firm belief is that it has been

saved by the good heart and good sense of Roworth the mayor, more
than by anything else: – if we are saved, for the Chartists have prepared a quantity of combustibles and are exceedingly ferocious. There
are quite enough of rascals amongst them to fire the town; and also
many good fellows so enraged at villany, such as I have described, as
to be ready for any violence, though they would regret it when they
saw what would happen.

  Both these classes are very dangerous, but the cowardice shewn is
absolutely ridiculous. One night, when out with 12 dragoons, a mob of
2000 followed and assailed us with abuse so violent as to make me fear
they would end with stones, a large heap being at hand. Thinking they
would have some respect for me, I told the magistrate and the dragoons
to ride on while I spoke to the mob, and I rode back alone. To my
surprise all fled, pushing each other down in their haste. At Sheffield
not a man faced the dragoons; fire and assassination are their weapons,
and now their nature, because they are driven to that course, the poor
law being the goad to keep them going. That law is however, in a
great measure, only new in name, for they give out-door relief
everywhere in the manufacturing districts; but they still separate
parents and children, which the people will not bear, and they are
right. The hatred to this law is not confined to Chartists, nor to the
poor, it creates Chartists, it makes them sanguinary; they mean to
spare no one that has a good coat if they once get to work: in short it is
all hell, or likely to be so in England.

Sir W. Napier, Life of General Sir Charles
James Napier (1857), ii.111-13

4 Chartism in Action

Thomas Cooper, who worked in Leicester as a journalist and edited the Chartist
Northern Counties Illuminator, was elected a delegate to the Chartist Conference
held at Manchester 1 August 1842. On his way to the conference he spoke at
several tumultuous Chartist meetings in Warwickshire and Staffordshire where
workmen were already out on strike. After his return to Leicester at the end of
the Conference he was one of the many Chartist leaders arrested and brought to
trial by the government.

'The Plug Plot', of 1842, as it is still called in Lancashire, began in
reductions of wages by the Anti-Corn-Law manufacturers, who did
not conceal their purpose of driving the people to desperation, in
order to paralyse the Government. The people advanced at last, to a

wild general strike, and drew the plugs so as to stop the works at the mills, and thus render labour impossible. Some wanted the men who spoke at the meetings held at the beginning of the strike to propose resolutions in favour of Corn Law Repeal; but they refused. The first meeting where the resolution was passed, 'that all labour should cease until the People's Charter became the law of the land', was held on the 7th of August, on Mottram Moor. In the course of a week, the resolution had been passed in nearly all the great towns of Lancashire, and tens of thousands had held up their hands in favour of it.

I constituted myself chairman of the meeting on the Crown Bank, at Hanley, on Monday morning, the 15th of August, 1842, a day to be remembered to my life's end. I resolved to take the chief responsibility on myself, for what was about to be done. I told the people so. I suppose there would be eight or ten thousand present. I showed them that if they carried out the resolution which was about to be proposed, no government on earth could resist their demand. But I told them that 'Peace, Law and Order' must be their motto; and that, while they took peaceable means to secure a general turn-out, and kept from violence, no law could touch them.

John Richards, who was seventy years of age and had been a member of the First Convention, – the oldest Chartist leader in the Potteries, – proposed the Resolution, 'That all labour cease until the People's Charter becomes the law of the land.'

A Hanley Chartist, whose name I forget, seconded it, and when I put the resolution to the crowd all hands seemed to be held up for it; and not one hand was held up when I said 'On the contrary.' Three cheers were given for success, and the meeting broke up. . . .

The day wore on, wearily, and very anxiously, till about five in the afternoon, when parties of men began to pass along the streets. Some came into my inn, and began to relate the history of the doings at Longton, which had been violent indeed. Yet the accounts they gave were confused, and I had still no clear understanding of what had been done.

By six o'clock, thousands crowded into the large open space about the Crown Inn, and instead of lecturing at eight o'clock in the room, the committee thought I had better go out at once, and lecture on the Crown Bank. So I went at seven o'clock to the place where I had stood in the morning. Before I began, some of the men who were drunk, and who, it seems, had been in the riot at Longton, came round me and wanted to shake hands with me. But I shook them off, and told them I was ashamed to see them. I began by telling the immense crowd – for its numbers were soon countless – that I had heard there had been destruction of property that day, and I warned all who had participated in that act, that they were not the friends, but the enemies of freedom – that ruin to themselves and others must attend this strike for the Charter, if they who pretended to be its advocates broke the law

'I proclaim Peace, Law, and Order!' I cried at the highest pitch of my voice. 'You all hear me; and I warn you of the folly and wrong you are committing, if you do not preserve Peace, Law, and Order!'

At dusk I closed the meeting; but I saw the people did not disperse; and two pistols were fired off in the crowd. No policeman had I seen the whole day! And what had become of the soldiers I could not learn. I went back to my inn; but I began to apprehend that mischief had begun which it would not be easy to quell. [Cooper left the same evening under cover of darkness.] My friends had purposely conducted me through dark streets, and led me out of Hanley in such a way that I saw neither spark, smoke, or flame. Yet the rioters were burning the houses of the Rev. Mr Aitken and Mr Parker, local magistrates, and the house of Mr Forrester, agent of Lord Granville (principal owner of the collieries in the Potteries) during that night. . . . Next morning thousands were again in the streets of Hanley and began to pour into the other Pottery towns from the surrounding districts. A troop of cavalry, under Major Beresford, entered the district and the daring colliers strove to unhorse the soldiers. Their commander reluctantly gave the order to fire; one man was killed at Burslem. The mob dispersed; but quiet was not restored until the day after this had been done, and scores apprehended and taken to prison. [After narrowly escaping arrest Burslem Cooper got away to Crewe to take a train to Manchester.]

When I entered the railway carriage at Crewe, some who were going to the Convention recognised me, – and, among the rest, Campbell, secretary of the 'National Charter Association'. He had left London on purpose to join the Conference; and, like myself, was anxious to know the *real* state of Manchester. So soon as the City of Long Chimneys came in sight, and every chimney was beheld smokeless, Campbell's face changed, and with an oath he said, 'Not a single mill at work! something must come out of this, and something serious too!'

In Manchester I soon found McDouall, Leach, and Bairstow, who, together with Campbell, formed what was called 'The Executive Council of the National Charter Association'. They said O'Connor was in Manchester and they hoped he would be at a meeting to be held that afternoon, at a public-house. He came to the place, but said it was not advisable to hold the Conference there: some better place must be had for the evening; and we had better separate. We all thought he seemed frightened.

In the streets, there were unmistakable signs of alarm on the part of the authorities. Troops of cavalry were going up and down the principal thoroughfares, accompanied by pieces of artillery, drawn by horses. In the evening, we held a meeting in the Reverend Mr Schofield's chapel, where O'Connor, the Executive, and a considerable number of delegates were present; and it was agreed to open the Conference, or Convention, in form, the next morning at nine o'clock. We met at that hour, the next morning, Wednesday, the 17th of August, when James Arthur of Carlisle was elected President. There were nearly sixty delegates present; and as they rose, in quick succession, to describe the state of their districts, it was evident they were, each and all, filled with the desire of keeping the people from returning to their labour. They believed the time had come for trying, successfully, to paralyse the Government. I caught their spirit – for the working of my mind had prepared me for it.

McDouall rose, after a while, and in the name of the Executive proposed, in form, that the Conference recommends the universal adoption of the resolution already passed at numerous meetings in Lancashire, – that all labour shall cease till the People's Charter becomes the law of the land. When the Executive, and a few others, had spoken, all in favour of the universal strike, I told the Conference I should vote for the resolution because it meant fighting, and I saw it must come to that. The spread of the strike would and must be followed by a general outbreak. The authorities of the land would try to quell it, but we must resist them. There was nothing now but a physical force struggle to be looked for. We must get the people out to fight; and they must be irresistable, if they were united.

[In the debate most of the delegates supported the strike for the same reasons as Cooper. On the other hand O'Connor deprecated any talk of fighting and William Hill, the editor of O'Connor's newspaper, the *Northern Star*, moved a resolution condemning the strike as merely playing into the hands of the Anti-Corn Law League.]

There were only six votes in favour of Editor Hill's amendment. O'Connor spoke late – evidently waiting to gather the spirit of the meeting before he voted with the majority, which he meant to do from the first. Yet he meant to do nothing in support of the strike, although he voted for it!

McDouall was a different kind of spirit. He hastily drew up an exciting and fiercely worded address to the working men of England, appealing to the God of Battles for the issue, and urging a universal strike. He got Leach to print this before the Convention broke up in the evening. The address was brought into the Convention, and Mc-Douall read the placard; but Editor Hill defiantly protested against it; and O'Connor moved that instead of its being sent out in the name of the Convention, the Executive should send it out in their own name. McDouall said the Executive would do so – and the Conference broke up.

Life of Thomas Cooper, written by himself (1879), pp. 190-211

5 Carlyle on the Condition of England Question

The Whig ministers who were in power during the first phase of Chartism were conscious of their traditional role of guardians of liberty rather than of order. Lord John Russell (Home Secretary 1835-9) deliberately minimised the seriousness of the disturbances, delayed arrests as long as possible, and preferred to allow mass meetings to take place as a method of blowing off the steam of popular discontent. Only at the very end of the 1839 session were the ministers sufficiently alarmed to ask parliament for an increase of 5,000 for the regular army, a rural police bill, and statutory power to set up efficient police forces at Birmingham, Manchester and Bolton. In the autumn of 1839, shortly before twenty-two Chartists were shot in a riot at Newport, Monmouthshire, the Attorney-General, Sir J. Campbell, claimed that the government had put down Chartism without spilling a drop of blood. Many Conservative politicians and members of the public on the other hand took the outbreaks more seriously, demanding firmer repressive measures, but at the same time sometimes showing greater concern than the Whigs for the underlying social and economic problems. Thomas Carlyle's pamphlet ('about the poor, their rights and their wrongs', as he described it) was written in the late autumn of 1839 and appeared at the end of the year. It received great interest, an edition of 1,000 copies being sold immediately. The allusions in it to 'Glasgow thuggery' refer to a notorious trial at Edinburgh in 1838 when five leading members of the Glasgow Operative Cotton Spinners Union were charged with conspiracy and murder. The evidence disclosed systematic intimidation of non-union spinners working for lower wages, by methods which included assault, vitriol-throwing, arson, shooting and assassination. A verdict of not-proven was returned on the major charges, guilty on the minor charges. The defendants were sentenced to seven years transportation but pardoned in 1840.

A feeling very generally exists that the condition and disposition of the Working Classes is a rather ominous matter at present; that something ought to be said, something ought to be done, in regard to it. And surely, at an epoch of history when the 'National Petition' carts itself in waggons along the streets, and is presented 'bound with iron hoops four men bearing it', to a reformed House of Commons; and Chartism numbered by the million and half, taking nothing by its iron-hooped Petition, breaks out into brickbats, cheap pikes, and even into sputterings of conflagration, such very general feeling cannot be considered unnatural! To us individually this matter appears, and has for many years appeared, to be the most ominous of all practical matters whatever; a matter in regard to which if something be not done, something will *do* itself one day, and in a fashion that will please nobody. The time is verily come for acting in it; how much more for consultation about acting in it, for speech and articulate inquiry about it!

We are aware that, according to the newspapers, Chartism is extinct; that a Reform Ministry has 'put down the chimera of Chartism' in the most felicitous effectual manner. So say the newspapers; – and yet, alas, most readers of newspapers know withal that it is indeed the 'chimera' of Chartism, not the reality, which has been put down. The distracted incoherent embodiment of Chartism, whereby in late months it took shape and became visible, this has been put down; or rather has fallen down and gone asunder by gravitation and law of nature: but the living essence of Chartism has not been put down. Chartism means the bitter discontent grown fierce and mad, the wrong condition therefore or the wrong disposition, of the Working Classes of England. It is a new name for a thing which has had many names, which will yet have many. The matter of Chartism is weighty, deep-rooted, far-extending; did not begin yesterday; will by no means end this day or to-morrow. Reform Ministry, constabulary rural police, new levy of soldiers, grants of money to Birmingham; all this is well, or is not well; all this will put down only the embodiment or 'chimera' of Chartism. The essence continuing, new and ever new embodiments, chimeras madder or less mad, have to continue. The melancholy fact remains, that this thing known at present by the name Chartism does exist; has existed; and, either 'put down', into secret treason, with rusty pistols, vitriol-bottle and match-box, or openly brandishing pike and torch (one knows not in which case *more* fatal-looking), is like to exist till quite other methods have been tried with it. What means this bitter discontent of the Working Classes? Whence comes it, whither goes it? Above all, at what price, on what terms, will it probably consent to depart from us and die into rest? These are questions.

To say that it is mad, incendiary, nefarious, is no answer. To say all this, in never so many dialects, is saying little. 'Glasgow Thuggery', 'Glasgow Thugs'; it is a witty nickname: the practice of 'Number 60' entering his dark room, to contract for and settle the price of blood with operative assassins, in a Christian city, once distinguished by its rigorous Christianism, is doubtless a fact worthy of all horror: but what will horror do for it? What will execration; nay at bottom, what will condemnation and banishment to Botany Bay do for it? Glasgow Thuggery, Chartist torch-meetings, Birmingham riots, Swing conflagrations, are so many symptoms on the surface; you abolish the symptom to no purpose, if the disease is left untouched. Boils on the surface are curable or incurable, – small matter which, while the virulent humour festers deep within; poisoning the sources of life; and certain enough to find for itself ever new boils and sore issues; ways of announcing that it continues there, that it would fain not continue there.

Delirious Chartism will not have raged entirely to no purpose, as indeed no earthly thing does so, if it have forced all thinking men of the community to think of this vital matter, too apt to be overlooked otherwise.

T. Carlyle, Chartism (1840), pp. 1-3

VI

THE CORN LAW AGITATION

1 The Corn Laws: Two Rival Petitions

In 1839 the cabinet had allowed both the ballot and the Corn Laws to become open questions and C. P. Villiers' motion for an enquiry into the Corn Laws though defeated was supported by a number of leading Whig ministers. In 1841 the 'freetrade' budget put forward by the government included the old Radical proposal for a moderate fixed duty on corn in place of the existing sliding scale. At the same time the formation of the Manchester Anti-Corn Law Association in 1838 followed next year by the national Anti-Corn Law League brought the issue before a wider public than that reached by the small group of free-trade Radicals in the House of Commons. Strictly speaking the government and the opposition were only disputing in 1841 over different degrees and methods of protection. But at the general election the popular cries of Free Trade, Cheap Bread, Big Loaf v. Little Loaf, roused much feeling on both sides. The two petitions which follow were presented at the first meeting of the new parliament. Of the two leading signatories James Bennett (1793-1872) of Cadbury House, Somerset, was a country squire and J. P.; Dr Pye Smith (1774-1851) was a prominent Congregationalist divine of moderate views who in previous years had tried to moderate Dissenting attacks on the Church.

(a) The Humble Petition of the undersigned, the Inhabitants of North and South Cadbury, in the county of Somerset,
 Sheweth,
 That we your Petitioners approach your honourable House under the most serious apprehension that the proposed alteration of the present Corn Law will be, if carried into effect, attended with dangerous consequences to the Nation, deluding the people with the expectation that cheap bread could be obtained without a corresponding lowering of wages, thereby raising hopes without the possibility of their being realised; that we consider that it is the first duty of the Legislature to ensure, as far as can be effected by human legislation, a certain, regular and sufficient supply of wheat for the consumption of the people, and that the present Corn Law effects that object as near as may be; in order that the supply of wheat may continue to be commensurate with

the utmost wants of the people, every security and encouragement must be afforded to home cultivation; that as experience has shown the uncertainty of commercial intercourse, it will be most ruinous to all ranks of society to place dependence upon foreign countries for the supply of wheat, instead of mainly relying on our native resources, thereby throwing our own labourers out of work, and risking the chance at a future day of famine in our now plenteous land.

That we further consider that uncertainty and vacillation in the Corn Laws are ruinous to the enterprize, skill, and outlay of the farmer, useless to the manufacturing classes, whose main stay is the home market; and that it is the greatest injustice to place the British agriculturist and those connected with the land, who are the great consumers of manufactured goods, on a par with the cultivators of foreign soils, who are comparatively unburthened with taxation and unacquainted with English comforts.

That it appears to your Petitioners fearful to contemplate the total disorganization of engagements, such as mortgages, settlement, annuitants, interests, or national securities, which must follow the depreciated value of our soil, at present bearing the principal weight of Parliament and local taxation.

That your petitioners humbly trust the funds of our charitable institutions may not be impaired, nor our moral or political importance as a nation be lessened; and that the agricultural interests of Britain may not be sacrificed or made secondary to any other interest whatever.

We your Petitioners humbly but strongly pray, that the existing Corn Laws may remain unaltered.

> James Bennett
> S. Blackall
> John Gifford
> &c. &c. &c.

(b) The humble Petition of the undersigned Members and Friends of the Congregation of Protestant Dissenters, assembling for divine worship in the Old Gravel Pit Meeting House at Hackney,

Sheweth,

That your Petitioners contemplate with pain and distressing apprehension the continuance of certain Laws of Her Majesty's realm, the design and effect of which are to restrict the supply of the necessaries of human life, and greatly to increase their cost.

That the results of those unhappy Laws are now made manifest in

the extreme sufferings of those classes of our fellow subjects which
constitute the basis of our national strength, in the depression of
manufactures, and their exportation to rival countries, in the miserabel
inadequate wages of both agricultural and manufacturing industry,
in the entire want of work to an alarming extent, in the hazardous and
pernicious direction given to mercantile pursuits, and in a fearful tendency to the impoverishing and ruin of the nation.

That your Petitioners are especially affected by a rational and
Christian conviction of the impiety involved in those Laws, as being in
their nature a crime against God, and as in their practical operation
productive of discontent, disloyalty, infidelity, profligacy of conduct, a
rejection of the authority of religion, and by necessary consequence the
most appealing dangers to the peace and security of all classes as to both
property and person.

That therefore your Petitioners humbly and earnestly implore your
honourable House to take these awful facts into your consideration, and
to adopt prompt and effectual measures to stop the progress of national
misery, and to prevent our common and irreparable ruin.

And your Petitioners shall ever pray.

> John Pye Smith, D.D. F.R.S.
> Minister
> John Jones
> Stephen Olding
> &c. &c. &c.

> *Votes and Proceedings of the House of Commons*
> (1841) (*Appendix to Reports of the Select Com-
> mittee on Public Petitions, 1841 session 2, nos
> 499, 568*)

2   Cobden on the Food-Tax, 1841

A feature of the early success of the League was its ability to reinforce the original
class effort of the manufacturers by harnessing the frustrated resentments of
Dissenters and radicals against the Church and aristocracy. As part of its activity
during and after the general election of 1841 a conference of seven hundred
ministers of religion carefully stage-managed by the League was held at
Manchester in August which passed a strong resolution condemning the Corn
Laws on moral and humanitarian grounds (cf. 1b above). It was to this that
reference is made in the speech quoted below. Cobden had already won a
position of importance in local Manchester politics and was a leading member

of the executive committee of the Anti-Corn Law Association which became in effect the governing body of the new League. He was returned for Stockport in the general election of 1841 and this extract is from his maiden speech in the debate on the Address. It was singled out for special praise to the Queen by Lord John Russell as 'a powerful speech from Mr Cobden, a manufacturer'. The use of the phrase 'Food-Tax' or 'Bread-Tax' was deliberately adopted by Cobden for its propaganda value. 'I think it is better to use the word bread-tax than the corn law,' he wrote to a correspondent in May 1840. 'A *bread-tax* is a good term to fix upon our opponents.'

He would take up but a moment of their time while he glanced at that great and paramount question which had been attempted to be cast aside. He alluded to the food-tax. The people of this country had been petitioning for three years. They were anxious for a total repeal of the food-tax. He spoke, too, in the utmost sincerity – he was also for a total and unconditional repeal of that tax. He would not allow an aspersion to be cast upon the three millions who had been petitioning for four years on this subject – he could not permit it to be said that they were not sincere in what they sought for. He knew that they were, because he knew that what they asked for was just. What was this bread-tax – this tax upon food and tax upon meat? . . . He had heard that tax called by a multitude of names. Some designated it as a 'protection'; but it was a tax after all, and he would call it nothing else. The bread tax was levied principally upon the working classes. He called the attention of the House to the working of the bread tax. The effect was this – it compelled the working classes to pay 40 per cent more, that is, a higher price than they should pay if there was a free trade in corn. When hon. Gentlemen spoke of 40s. as the price of foreign corn, they would make the addition 50 per cent. He would not over state the case, and therefore he set down the bread tax as imposing an additional tax of 40 per cent. He had now to call their attention to facts contained in the report of the Committee on the hand-loom weavers. It was a report got up with great care, and singular talent. It gave, amongst other things, the amount of the earnings of a working man's family, and that was put down at 10s. Looking at the metropolitan and rural districts, they found that not to be a bad estimate of the earnings of every labouring family. The hand-loom committee then stated that out of the 10s. every family expended in the week 5s. in bread. Their tax upon that was 2s. weekly, so that every man who had 10s. weekly, gave out of that 2s. to the bread-tax. That was twenty per cent. out of the income of every labouring family. But let them proceed upward, and see how the same tax worked. The man who had

20s. a week, still paid 2s. a week to the bread tax; that was to him ten
per cent, as an income tax. If they went further – to the man who had
40s. a week – the income tax upon him in this way was five per cent. If
they mounted higher – to the man who had £1. a week, or 250l. a year –
it was one per cent. income tax. Let them ascend to the nobility and
the millionaires, to those who had an income of 200,000l. a year. His
family was the same as that of the poor man, and how did the bread-tax
affect him? It was one halfpenny in every 100l. . . . And yet there was
the tax which was actually levied, not for the purposes of the state, but
for the benefit of the richest of the community. This, he apprehended,
was a fair statement of the working and effect of the tax on bread. . . .

The House had heard of the condition of the labouring population
in the north. He had lately had an opportunity of seeing a report
of the state of our labouring population in all parts of the country
Probably hon. Gentlemen were aware that a very important meeting
had lately been held at Manchester, he alluded to the meeting of the
ministers of religion. [A laugh.] He understood that laugh, but he
should not pause in his statement of facts, but might perhaps notice it
before concluding. He had seen a body of ministers of religion of all
denominations – 650, and not thirty in number – assembled from all
parts of the country, at an expense of from three to four thousand
pounds, paid by their congregations. At that meeting most important
statements of facts were made relating to the condition of the labouring
classes. He would not trouble the House by reading those statements,
but they showed, that in every district of the country – and these
statements rested upon unimpeachable authority – the condition of the
great body of her Majesty's labouring population had deteriorated
woefully within the last ten years, and more especially within the last
three years, and that in proportion as the price of food increased, in
the same proportion the comforts of the working classes had diminished.
One word with respect to the manner in which his allusion to this
meeting was received. He did not come there to vindicate the conduct
of these Christian men in having assembled in order to take this subject
into consideration. The parties who had to judge them were their own
congregations There were at that meeting members of the Established
Church, of the Church of Rome, Independents, Baptists, members of the
Church of Scotland, and of the Secession Church, Methodists, and,
indeed, ministers of every other denomination, and if he were disposed
to impugn the character of those divines, he felt he should be casting a
stigma and a reproach upon the great body of professing Christians in
this country. . . . Those reverend Gentlemen had prepared and signed a

petition, in which they prayed for the removal of those laws – laws which, they stated, violated the Scriptures, and prevented famishing children from having a portion of those fatherly bounties which were intended for all people: and he would remind honourable Gentlemen that, besides these 650 ministers, there were 1,500 others, from whom letters had been received, offering up their prayers in their several localities to incline the will of Him who ruled princes and potentates to turn your hearts to justice and mercy. When they found so many ministers of religion, without any sectarian differences, joining heart and hand in a great cause, there could be no doubt of their earnestness. He begged to call to their minds whether these worthy men would not make very efficient ministers in this great cause? They knew what they had done in the anti-slavery question, when the religious public was roused; and what the difference was between stealing a man, and making him labour, and robbing a man of the fruit of his industry, he could not perceive. The noble Lord, the Member of North Lancashire, knew something of the abilities of those men. The noble Lord had told the House that from the moment the religious community and their pastors took up the question of slavery, from that moment the agitation must be successful. He believed this would be the case in the present instance.

Hansard, lix.235-42 (25 August 1841)

3 Peel on the Corn Laws, 1841

In fiscal policy Peel was in the liberal tradition of Pitt, Liverpool, Huskisson and Robinson. He had been a leading member in the government of 1828 which had abandoned the principle of absolute exclusion of foreign corn up to a certain price and returned to the principle of a sliding scale. In the 1830s his attitude was that agriculture along with the other great interests should receive adequate protection, especially in view of the special burdens on the land, land-tax, tithe, poor-rate and malt-tax. But he did not accept that the landowners should be regarded as a favoured body for whom the rest of the community should be taxed and he believed that the interests of industry and agriculture were interdependent. His support of agricultural protection was therefore based on expediency; he did not give it prominence; and he reserved his right to modify the existing law when he came to power. In fact in 1842, as one of his first major acts of legislation, he passed a new Corn Law almost halving the previous scale of protection, though retaining the principle of a sliding scale as a more flexible device than a fixed duty, especially in time of scarcity.

I now approach the more important and exciting question of the

Corn-laws. In order that I may make no mistake, allow me to refer to the expressions which I made use of on this point before the dissolution. I said, that on consideration I had formed an opinion, which intervening consideration has not induced me to alter, that the principle of a gradual scale was preferable to that of a fixed and irrevocable duty; but I said then, and I say now, in doing so I repeat the language which I held in 1839, that I will not bind myself to the details of the existing law, but will reserve to myself the unfettered discretion of considering and amending that law. I hold the same language now; but if you ask me whether I bind myself to the maintenance of the existing law in its details, or if you say that that is the condition in which the agricultural interest give me their support, I say that on that condition I will not accept their support. . . . If I could bring myself to think – if I could believe that an alteration of the Corn-laws would preclude the risk of such distress – if I thought it would be an effectual remedy, in all cases, against such instances of lamentable suffering as that which have been described, I would say at once to the agricultural interest, 'It is for your advantage rather to submit to any reduction of price, than, if an alteration of the Corn-laws would really be the cure for these sufferings, to compel their continuance.' I should say, that it would be for the interest, not of the community in general, but especially of the agriculturists themselves, if, by any sacrifice of theirs, they could prevent the existence of such distress. If any sacrifice of theirs could prevent their being the real cause of the distress – could prevent the continuance of it – could offer a guarantee against the recurrence of it, I would earnestly advise a relaxation, an alteration, nay, if necessary, a repeal of the Corn-laws. But it is because I cannot convince my mind that the Corn-laws are at the bottom of this distress, or that the repeal of them, or the alteration of their principle, would be its cure, that I am induced to continue my maintenance of them. . . .

Hansard lix.,413-29 (27 August 1841

4 A Conservative Attack on the Anti-Corn Law League

After the first successes the Anti-Corn Law League lost its momentum, especially when Peel introduced his free-trade budget, the income tax, and the corn bill in the spring of 1842, all of which received a considerable amount of middle-class support. To keep up the agitation various extreme measures were considered.

by the League leaders. There was discussion of a plan to refuse payment of taxes until the corn laws were repealed; Cobden thought that every effort should be made to discredit parliament and embarrass the government; Bright and others advocated a scheme for manufacturers to close down their factories and produce unemployment in order to force the government's hand. The acute industrial distress of the 1841-2 period provided a strong temptation to the League to exploit working-class disorder and the danger was greater since in many manufacturing towns the bulk of the magistrates were Leaguers. The Plug Plot of August 1842 (see **V**, **4**) was, however, a strike by workmen against wage-reductions and it was the Chartists and not the Leaguers who took advantage of the situation. Nevertheless League lecturers had been busy stirring up feeling in the affected areas and it was alleged both by Chartists and sections of the Tory press that the League had taken a hand in promoting the strikes and lock-outs. There was in fact, as the government realised, no evidence of this, though Peel and Graham were dissatisfied at the conduct of some of the magistrates and held the League morally responsible for much of the disturbances. At Peel's request the Home Office collected a dossier on the activities of the League and this was eventually handed over to J. W. Croker to work up in article form for the *Quarterly Review*. The article, extracts from which are given here, appeared in December 1842. The Conference at which Cobden made the speeches quoted was one of Anti-Corn Law delegates meeting in London as a kind of rival body to Parliament.

We now proceed to Mr Cobden's appearance in the Conference of the 11th of February, 1842. Mr Cobden on that occasion said – '*That three weeks would try the mettle of his countrymen (hear, hear)*. Why, would they submit to be starved, and put upon short allowance, by thirty or forty thousand men? (*Loud cries of No, no.*) He was sure that if they knew how insignificant, both morally and *physically*, those thirty thousand or forty thousand aristocrats and squires were, they would not fear them (*Hear, hear*). But though really insignificant, they were not conscious of any weakness; they were as confident in their strength as they had been five years since; they would not shrink one atom; *and until these men were frightened the people would never obtain justice*. . . .

'Were they prepared to make sacrifices, and to undergo sufferings to carry this question? (*Cheers, and loud cries of Yes, yes.*) *The time was not far off when they might be called upon to make sacrifices, and to undergo sufferings.* The time might soon come when they might be called upon to inquire, *as Christian men*, whether an *oligarchy* which has usurped the government (*Cheers*), *placed its foot on the Crown* (*Immense cheering, which continued some minutes*), and trampled down the people (*Continued cheering*). – how far such *an oligarchical usurpation* was deserving of their moral and religious support (*Immense cheering*). . . . As soon as the bill should become the law of the land, *by the physical force of a brute majority against reason*, then would the time come when he should feel it his duty to secede, as far as he could do morally, from giving all voluntary support, whether *pecuniary* or morally, to such a government (*Here the whole meeting rose, waving their hats, and cheering for several minutes*). The administrators of the law might enforce the law – he would not resist the law – but there must be somebody to administer the law, and somebody to enforce the law; and he thought *that three weeks hence* the whole people would so thoroughly understand the real bearings of this bread-tax question, that they would *not want physical force while they were unanimous* (*Loud cheers*).'. . . .

Meanwhile, the Conference continued its daily exercise of agitation; and on the 12th July Mr Cobden appeared there in person, and made a speech – which, coming from a man in his station, and conveyed, with the applauses of a hired press, to an excited populace, was well calculated to produce awful mischief, though in other circumstances, its intrinsic nonsense would have only excited contempt.

He said amongst a variety of similar ebullitions, – 'Whatever they could do to embarrass the Government they were bound to do. They owed them no respect: they were entitled to none. They owed them no service which they could possibly avoid. *The Government was based upon corruption, and the offspring of VICE, CORRUPTION, VIOLENCE, INTIMIDATION, and BRIBERY. The majority of the House of Commons was supported by the violation of morality and religion. He said for such a Government they should entertain no respect whatever. He would assist the Anti-Corn-Law League all in his power to embarrass the Government*.'. . .

We are satisfied that we have made out such a case against the Anti-Corn-Law Association and League, as no rational man in the country. . . can resist.

We have shown that these societies set out with a public and fundamental engagement to act by '*legal and constitutional means*'; but that, on the contrary, all their proceedings have been in the highest degree *unconstitutional*, and, to the common sense of mankind, *illegal*.

We have shown that their second fundamental engagement, that '*no party political discussion should be allowed at any of their meetings*', has been scandalously violated; and that the *language* of their speeches and their press has been not merely *violent* and *indecent* – but incendiary and seditious.

We have shown that, even from the outset, they endeavoured to menace the government and the legislature with the pressure of *physical force*, and that these threats continued with increasing violence, till lost at length in the tumult of the actual outbreak which they had provoked.

We have shown that the *Magistrates* who belonged to these societies, instead of maintaining the peace and tranquillity of their respective jurisdictions, were amongst the most prominent and violent promoters of every species of agitation; and that, while all of them talked language and promulgated doctrines that endangered the public peace, some, the highest in authority, volunteered declarations which those inclined to disturb the public peace might reasonably consider as promises of, at least, impunity.

We have shown that the League have spent, according to their own statement, 90,000l. in the last year, we know not exactly how, but clearly in furtherance of the unconstitutional, illegal, and dangerous practices which we have detailed.

We have shown, we think, abundant reason to conclude that the 50,000l. which they are now endeavouring to raise is probably destined to the same, or perhaps still more illegal, unconstitutional, and dangerous practices.

We have shown that – from first to last – their system has been one of falsehood and deception – from their original fundamental imposture of being the advocates of the *poor* – down to the meaner shifts of calling brutal violence freedom of discussion, and a subscription for feeding sedition and riot a fund for education or charity.

And, finally, we hope we have shown that no man of common sense of any party – if he only adheres to the general principles of the British Constitution – can hesitate to pronounce the existence of such associations – *raising money* – *exciting mobs* – *organized* – and – to use a term of the same Jacobin origin as their own, *affiliated* – for the avowed purpose of coercing the government and the legislature – can hesitate, we say, to pronounce the existence of such associations disgraceful to our national character, and wholly incompatible either with the internal peace and commercial prosperity of the country – or, in the highest meaning of the words – the SAFETY OF THE STATE.

Quarterly Review, lxxi, art. on Anti-Corn Law Agitation (Dec. 1842)

5 The Power-House of the League: Newall's Buildings, 1843

Alexander Somerville, former trooper in the Scots Greys, an ex-Chartist, and a brilliant if alcoholic journalist, was recruited by Cobden as one of several authors and publicists who posed as independent observers of the social and political scene while being in the secret pay of the League. Somerville contributed a series of articles, mainly aimed at agricultural readers, which appeared in the *Morning Chronicle* under the pseudonym of *The Whistler at the Plough* from 1847 on. This description of the headquarters of the League was dated January 1843; and gives a clear picture of the skill and organisation which the business-men of the League brought to its activities. The articles were published by Somerville in collected form in 1852 with a somewhat garbled version of his connection with Cobden and the League.

Having a day to spend in Manchester, . . . I determined to get a peep, if possible, at that extraordinary body the Anti-Corn-Law League. . . .

Accordingly, at ten o'clock I was in Market Street, a principal thoroughfare in Manchester. A wide open stairway, with shops on each side of its entrance, rises from the level of the pavement, and lands on the first floor of a very extensive house called 'Newall's Buildings'. The house consists of four floors, all of which are occupied by the League, save the basement. We must, therefore, ascend the stair, which is wide enough to admit four or five persons walking abreast.

On reaching a spacious landing, or lobby, we turn to the left, and, entering by a door, see a counter somewhere between forty and fifty feet in length, behind which several men and boys are busily employed, some registering letters in books, some keeping accounts, some folding and addressing newspapers, others going out with messages and parcels. This is the general office, and the number of persons here employed is, at the present time, ten. Beyond this is the *Council Room*, which, for the present, we shall leave behind and go up stairs to the second floor.

Here we have a large room, probably forty feet by thirty, with a table in the centre running lengthwise, with seats around for a number of persons, who meet in the evenings, and who are called the 'Manchester Committee' . . .

During the day this room is occupied by those who keep the accounts of cards issued and returned to and from all parts of the kingdom. A professional accountant is retained for this department, and a committee of members of council give him directions and inspect his books. These books are said to be very ingeniously arranged, so as to shew at a glance the value of the cards sent out, their value being represented by certain alphabetical letters and numbers, the names and residences of the parties to whom sent, the amounts of deficiencies of those returned, and so on.

Passing from this room we come to another, from which all the correspondence is issued. From this office letters to the amount of several thousands a-day go forth to all parts of the kingdom. While here, I saw letters addressed to all the foreign ambassadors, and all the mayors and provosts of corporate towns of the United Kingdom, inviting them to the great banquet which is to be given in the last week of this month. . . . In this office copies of all the parliamentary registries of the kingdom are kept, so that any elector's name and residence is at once found, and, if necessary, such elector is communicated with by letter or parcel of tracts, irrespective of the committees in his own district.

Passing from this apartment, we see two or three small rooms, in which various committees of members of the council meet. Some of these committees are permanent, some temporary. Of those which are permanent I may name that for receiving all applications for lecturers and deputations to public meetings. . . .

In another large room on this floor is the packing department. Here several men are at work making up bales of tracts, each weighing upwards of a hundred weight, and despatching them to all parts of the kingdom for distribution among the electors. From sixty to seventy of these bales are sent off in a week, that is, from three to three and a-half tons of arguments against the corn-Laws! . . .

Leaving this and going to the floor above, we find a great number of printers, presses, folders, stitchers, and others connected with printing, at work. But in addition to the printing and issuing of tracts here, the League has several other printers at work in this and other towns of the Kingdom. Altogether they have twelve master-printers employed, one of whom, in Manchester, pays upwards of L.100 a-week in wages for League work alone.

A. Somerville, *The Whistler at the Plough*
(1852), pp. 79-82

6   An Anti-League Pamphlet

The attacks of the League on the agricultural interest soon began to evoke counter-measures by farmers and gentry, particularly after 1842 when the

League extended its missionary efforts to the rural areas. Agricultural Protection Societies were formed in many counties and in February 1844 they were given national leadership by the Central Agricultural Protection Society for the United Kingdom set up under the presidency of the Duke of Richmond with the Duke of Buckingham as vice-president and a number of great peers as trustees. The main work of this 'Anti-League' organisation was to agitate for the continuance of protection, counter the activities of the League in the country districts, and bring pressure to bear on local M.P.s. This influential network of local and national associations provided the driving-force behind most of the opposition to Peel inside the Conservative party in 1846. In addition numbers of pamphlets appeared on the protectionist side, especially in 1843-4. The protectionists sought to discredit their opponents by using material from the reports of enquiries into factory conditions and quoting the virulent language of League attacks on landowners and tenants. Intellectually a more cogent line was the exposure of the inconsistencies and contradictions in League statements about the effect of repeal on prices and wages. The pamphlet quoted below, which made effective use of this tactic, obtained wide publicity and by 1844 had run into twelve editions.

The Anti-Corn-Law League was instituted at Manchester, in 1839, and has since extended its ramifications from its original depot to every corner of England. The tact of its leaders is, to magnify present evils to those immediately suffering under them, and to delude the sufferers by assigning false grounds for the existence of such evils. . . . Hence, for this alone they pronounce the landlords to be all that is base in honour, – brutal in feeling, – and wicked in morals![1]

Their conduct shows, that they have no dignified love of truth, – no serious wish for fair discussion; but seek every opportunity to interrupt and silence rather than to hear, an opponent. . . . And what good does the League expect to accomplish for all the enormous sums which it has obtained, and is obtaining, from the public?

The following *answers* which I place in juxta-position, are from the Leaguers themselves: –

The League Oracle[2] says –	Mr Cobden says –
I. 'If we have free trade, the landlord's rents will fall 100%.' (League Circular, No. 15, p. 3.) (ibid. No. 12.)	I. 'If we have free trade, the landlords will have as good rents as now.' (Speech in the House of Commons, 15 May last.)

[1] The following are a few of the epithets which this self-styled Holy League, in what they call their 'labour of love', bestow on the landlords: 'Monsters of impiety', 'relentless demons', 'heartless brutes', 'rapacious harpies', 'merciless footpads', 'inhuman fiends' 'swindlers', 'plunderers of the people', 'murderers'.

[2] The Anti-Corn-Law Circular.

II. 'provisions will fall one-third.' – (League Circular, No. 34, p. 4) 'The Corn Law makes the labourer pay double the price for his food.' – (League Circular, No. 15.)

II. 'Provisions will be no cheaper.' (Speech at Bedford, Hertford Reformer, 10th June last.)

III. 'The Corn Law compels us to pay three times the value for a loaf of bread.' – (League Circular, No. 13.) ... 'In the American port of Cincinnati alone, there are a million of quarters of wheat which we could purchase at 16s.; – or less than one-fourth the price which we are now compelled to pay for our home-grown product.' – (League Circular, No. 39.)

III. 'The argument for cheap bread was never mine.' (Morning Chronicle, 30th June 1843, Speech on Penenden Heath.) 'The idea of low-priced foreign corn is all a delusion.' (Speech at Winchester, Salisbury Herald, July 29, 1843, p. 3.) ...

IV. Messrs Villiers, Muntz, Hume, Roche, Thornton, Rawson, Sandars, (all avowed Free Traders) say, and the oracle of the League itself has said, that 'We want free trade, to enable us to reduce wages, that we may compete with foreigners.' – (Speech, pp. 13-16.)

IV. Messrs Cobden, Bright, and Moore, now affirm – 'It is a base falsehood to say we want free trade to enable us to reduce the rate of wages.' – (Mr Cobden on Penenden Heath. Messrs Bright and Moore at Huntingdon.)

V. The League Oracle admits that 'a repeal would injure the farmer, but not so much as he fears.' (League Circular, No. 58.)

V. Cobden, Moore, and Bright, say, that it is to the interest of the farmer to have a total and immediate repeal. – (Uxbridge, Bedford, Huntingdon.)

Thus, it will be seen that, upon the MOST VITAL POINTS, – points that have deluded thousands of their present votaries, – the Leaguers contradict themselves. They have been guilty of contradictions, such as would nonsuit any cause in any Court where Common Honesty sat as Judge! ...

Is it not the *duty* of every man, who desires peace and prosperity to his country, to arouse himself, and oppose a League so founded, – so conducted, – so mischievous, as this? I feel that, in this case, at least, the fetters of party ought to be broken; and that honourable men, *of all shades of political opinion*, should join together, as one man, to resist a confederacy which is inimical to the peace and the interests of our common country.

Defeat of the Anti-Corn-Law League in Huntingdonshire: The Speech of Mr George Game Day (London, 1844). From the Introduction written by the speaker.

[The speech was originally delivered at a meeting at Huntingdon on 17 June 1843 addressed by Bright and Moore on behalf of the League which was completely unsuccessful largely owing to the intervention of Day, a Whig country gentleman of St. Ives. It was followed by the formation of an Anti-League Association for Huntingdonshire in January 1844.]

VII

THE REPEAL OF THE CORN LAWS

1 The Irish Peasant and the Potato

Since the end of the eighteenth century a large part of the rural Irish population had become dependent on a single food crop – the potato. The precariousness of this situation had been demonstrated in 1817 during Peel's Irish Secretaryship. In 1816 occurred the first major failure of the crop. It was followed next year by near-famine conditions accompanied by typhus. In 1822 and 1826 (while Peel was Home Secretary) there were further administrative crises in Ireland because of food-shortages, though they were less severe than in 1817. When therefore the potato disease, which was already affecting large areas of the Continent, appeared in the United Kingdom in the autumn of 1845, it was clear that the chief contingent threat was to Ireland. The danger was greater since the potato blight (a fungus disease) was virtually unknown to British and European scientists. They were unable to discover its precise nature and were unable consequently to infer appropriate remedies. It was in fact another generation before it was definitely diagnosed. Two years before the disease struck Ireland a Royal Commission under the chairmanship of the Earl of Devon had been set up to enquire into the law and practice of land occupation in Ireland. Its Report with appendices and evidence was published in four large volumes in February 1845 (P. P. 1845 XIX-XXII). A Digest of its conclusions and evidence was subsequently published in 1847. The first extract is from the introductory remarks in ch.1 'On Agriculture', written by the Secretary to the Commission, Captain Kennedy, after the outbreak of the disease. The second is from the original 1845 report of the Commissioners (generally known as the Devon Report) which was reprinted in the Digest.

(a) It has been stated almost universally throughout the evidence, that the lands in nearly every district of Ireland require drainage; that the drainage and deep moving of the lands or subsoiling have proved most remunerative operations wherever they have been applied; that these operations have as yet been introduced but to a very limited extent.

That the mass of the lands is held by small working farmers.

That the small farmers and labourers are for considerable portions of the year in search of employment which they cannot obtain.

That the most valuable crops and the most profitable rotations cannot be adopted on wet lands, &c., &c.

These apparent contradictions are variously accounted for by different witnesses. Some attributing the apathy that exists to want of capital, which they strongly recommend to be supplied in some way or other. But this cause would not prevent the small farmer from draining the wet field of which he is the occupier, and which is situated at his own door, instead of sitting idle for several months of the year, and complaining all the while that he cannot find profitable employment!

Others, and by far the most extensive class of witnesses, attribute the inertia to the fact of the occupiers not having any certainty of receiving compensation, if removed immediately after having effected valuable improvements; and to their not generally having leases, or that security of tenure of their farms which would justify them in expending labour or money in their improvement, as, if they did so, the proprietor would then have the power of immediately increasing the rent. . . .

A close analysis of this subject would probably lead to the conclusion, that the potato is the main cause of that inertia in the population, and that want of improvement in the lands and tillage, which is so striking throughout Ireland.

This root, as compared with other food stuffs grown in this climate, supplied the largest amount of human food on the smallest surface. Its peculiar cultivation enabled the occupier of land to plant it in the wettest soils; because the ridge or lazy bed, universally adopted in such cases, supplied the most minute system of drainage that can be imagined for that one crop, although it did not permanently drain the land, or extend any substantial benefit in that respect even to the following crop.

The indolent occupier, therefore, passed his winter inactively, consuming this food which he preferred to all others, and neglecting to prepare his land permanently for more profitable crops, of which he had heard little, and for which he cared less. Enjoying all the while the pleasing delusion, that, as sure as the spring came round, any portion he might select of his farm would be ready to receive his favourite root, and to furnish a certain supply of food for his numerous and increasing family.

Digest of Evidence on Occupation of Land in Ireland (1847), Pt. I, 14-16

LABOURERS

(b) We must not omit to notice the system which prevails in a greater
or less degree in every part of Ireland, of letting land for one or more
crops, commonly known as the con-acre system. The land so let is in
some few districts called quarter land or rood land.

Much has been said in condemnation of this system; but still we are
convinced that some practice of this nature is essential to the comfort,
almost the existence, of the Irish peasant. Under ordinary circumstances
the wages of his labour alone will not enable him to purchase food and
other necessaries, and to pay even the most moderate rent. It becomes
therefore necessary that he should resort to some other means for
procuring subsistence, and these can only be found in the occupation of
a piece of ground which shall furnish a crop of potatoes for food. This
he generally takes from some farmer in the neighbourhood, upon
conditions which vary much according to the particular terms of
agreement respecting the ploughing, the manure, the seed, &c.

Although the taker of con-acre ground may, in ordinary years,
receive a good return for the rent which he assumes, yet, as the
amount of such rent, although not unreasonable in respect of the
farmer's expenditure upon the land, is always large with reference to
the ordinary means of a labourer, a bad season, and a failure in the
crops, leave the latter in a distressed condition, subject to a demand
which he is wholly unable to meet.

Ibid., Pt. II (Report of the Commissioners),
1151-2

2 Peel's Cabinet Memorandum, 1 November 1845

In mid-October, when reports of the progress of the potato-blight in Ireland
were becoming serious, the prime minister sent across two scientists, John
Lindley, professor of botany at London University, and Lyon Playfair, an
eminent chemist, to confer with local experts, report on the disease and suggest
possible remedies. From their initial reports it was clear that the danger was
greater than the general public realised and that immediate steps should be
taken to prepare for famine conditions especially in the late winter and spring.
The cabinet met on 31 October to hear all the information gathered by the
Home Office and on 1 November the prime minister read to them the memorandum from which the extracts are taken. In the discussions which followed
serious differences of opinion showed themselves. At a further meeting on 6
November only three members of the cabinet (Graham, Aberdeen and Herbert)

supported Peel's proposal to suspend immediately by order in council the duties on grain, summon parliament at the end of the month, and announce that the government would bring forward a bill after Christmas to modify the existing corn law. The rest of the cabinet were either opposed in principle to any change in the law or not convinced that the danger warranted such a step.

If we can place confidence in the Reports which we have received, there is the prospect of a lamentable deficiency of the ordinary food of the people in many parts of Ireland, and in some parts of this country, and of Scotland. The evil *may be* much greater than present reports lead us to anticipate. Potatoes which now appear safe may become infected, and we must not exclude from our consideration the contingency of a great calamity. . . .

With the documents we have in our possession, with the opinions of our own Commissioners as to the probable extent of the evil, the pressing entreaties from the Lord-Lieutenant for instructions, the possible contingency that in the course of two months the evil may prove to have been much more extensive than any one has yet contemplated, inaction and indifference might involve the country in serious danger, and the Government in the heaviest responsibility.

I recommend, therefore, that we should in the first place adopt some such measures as were adopted at former periods of much more partial scarcity – that we should authorise the Lord-Lieutenant to appoint a Commission for the purpose of considering the mode in which relief, when necessary, can be applied, through the means of employment where employment can be had. . . .

It appears to me that the adoption of these measures, the advance or promise of public money to provide food or employ labour, on account of apprehended scarcity of food, will compel the assembling of Parliament before Christmas. . . .

I cannot disguise from myself that the calling together of Parliament on account of apprehended scarcity – the prohibition of export in other countries – the removal of restrictions on import (sanctioned, as in the case of Belgium, by an unanimous vote of the Chambers) – the demand for public money, to be applied to provide sustenance for a portion of the people – will constitute a great crisis, and that it will be dangerous for the Government, having assembled Parliament, to resist with all its energies any material modification of the Corn Law.

By material modification I mean of the law as it applies to the import of barley, oats, and wheat.

There are reasons – very good ones, under ordinary circumstances – for dealing specially with colonial grain, or with maize, or with rice;

but I greatly fear that partial and limited interference with the Corn
Law, under the circumstances under which Parliament will assemble
(if it be assembled) at the latter end of this month, will be no solution of
our difficulties.

Supposing it were granted to me, for the purpose of argument, that
the suspension of the Corn Law is inevitable, the question arises, shall
the suspension take place by an act of prerogative, or by legislation at
the instance of the Government?

In favour of suspension by prerogative, there is the argument that
it is done at once, that it is decisive for the time, that it prevents all
that suspense and stagnation which will follow the notoriety of facts as
to the potato crop, the meetings of the Cabinet, the notice in a few
days of the summoning of Parliament.

It gives the earliest notice in foreign countries, and it gives to the
proceeding the character of an act done on an urgent necessity, which
no human foresight could have guarded against.

The objections to it are – that it compels instant decision by the
Cabinet – that it imposes upon us the necessity of proving that there
could be no delay.

It may justly be said, Parliament, after much deliberation, sanctioned
an elaborate and comprehensive system of Corn Laws. The Crown has
the power to summon Parliament by a notice of fourteen days. Why
should the Crown, by the stroke of a pen, abrogate laws so fully
considered by Parliament, instead of summoning Parliament at the
earliest period, and inviting Parliament to do that which it is the proper
province of Parliament to do?

There is this advantage also in doing whatever it may be necessary to
do in the ordinary constitutional mode.

It gives us some further time for consideration.

It is possible for us to take this course – to separate to-day under the
strong impression that the meeting of Parliament on some day not
later than the 27th of November is inevitable – to have a meeting of the
Cabinet finally to decide our course at the latter end of next week.

If we then resolve on calling Parliament, to fix the day for the Council
at which the day of meeting for the despatch of business shall be determined.

This course is possible, but it leaves unaltered the necessity of de-
termining, before we resolve on calling Parliament, the course we shall
pursue. We must make our choice between determined maintenance,
modification, and suspension of the existing Corn Law.

In writing the above I have merely considered the question on its own abstract merits, without reference to mere party considerations, or our own position as public men, the authors of the present Corn Law. I am fully aware of the gravity of the considerations connected with this part of the question.

ROBERT PEEL

Peel *Memoirs*, ii.141-8

3   A Colleague's Misgivings

After the inconclusive meetings of early November, the cabinet agreed to meet again at the end of the month, when Peel had made up his mind to resign if he could not get the full support of his colleagues. Meanwhile reports from Ireland grew steadily worse and in the middle of the month he arranged for the secret purchase of large quantities of maize from America through the merchant banking house of Baring. On 22 November Lord John Russell wrote from Edinburgh an open letter to his constituents in the City of London announcing his conversion to a policy of total repeal of the Corn Laws and calling on the public for an immediate agitation for their removal. The cabinet met three days later and approved detailed instructions to the Lord Lieutenant of Ireland on measures to meet the now certain famine. On the 26th Peel read a second memorandum to the cabinet stating that he could not consent to the issue of these instructions and at the same time undertake the maintenance of the existing corn laws. Suspension was now in his view inevitable and this in turn made necessary a critical review of the whole question of corn protection. A third supporting memorandum was circulated on 29 November which evoked replies from several ministers, including the following from Henry Goulburn, chancellor of the exchequer. Most of them showed a reluctance on various grounds, economic and political, to accept Peel's proposals though also an unwillingness to see him retire from office.

Mr GOULBURN to Sir R. PEEL.
(Private and confidential)

Downing Street, Sunday evening,
[30 November 1845]

MY DEAR PEEL,

I have such an habitual deference to the superiority of your judgment and such an entire confidence in the purity of your motives, that I always feel great doubt as to my being right when I differ from you in opinion. But the more I reflect upon the observations which you made to me a few days since as to your difficulty in again defending a

Corn Law in Parliament, the more do I feel alarmed at the consequences of your taking a different course from that which you have
previously adopted. An abandonment of your former opinions now
would, I think, prejudice your and our characters as public men, and
would be fraught with fatal results to the country's best interests; and
as I probably hear many opinions on a subject of this kind which do
not reach you, the view which I take of probable consequences may
not be undeserving of consideration – at least you will not misinterpret
my motives in stating it.

I fairly own that I do not see how the repeal of the Corn Law is to
afford relief to the distress with which we are threatened. I quite
understand that if we had never had a Corn Law, it might be argued
that we should now have had a larger supply in our warehouses, or
that from the encouragement given by a free trade in corn to the growth
of it in foreign countries, we should have had a larger fund on which to
draw for a supply. But I think it next to impossible to show that the
abandonment of the law now could materially affect this year's supply,
or give us any corn which will not equally reach us under the law as it
stands. . .

Under these circumstances it appears to me that the abandonment of
the Corn Law would be taken by the public generally as decisive
evidence that we never intended to maintain it further than as an instrument by which to vex and defeat our enemies. The very caution with
which we have spoken on the subject of corn will confirm this impression. Had we always announced a firm determination under all circumstances to uphold the Corn Law, it would have been more readily
believed that in abandoning it now we were yielding to the pressure of
an overwhelming necessity which we did not before anticipate. But
when the public feel, as I believe they do, great doubts as to the existence
of an adequate necessity – when greater doubts still are entertained as to
the applicability of the abandonment of the Corn Law as a remedy to
the present distress – they will, I fear, with few dissentient voices, tax us
with treachery and deception, and charge us, from our former language,
with having always had it in contemplation.

So much as to the effect on our character as public men. But I view
with greater alarm its effects on public interests. In my opinion the
party of which you are the head is the only barrier which remains
against the revolutionary effects of the Reform Bill. So long as that
party remains unbroken, whether in or out of power, it has the means
of doing much good, or at least of preventing much evil. But if it be
broken in pieces by a destruction of confidence in its leaders (and I

cannot but think that an abandonment of the Corn Law would produce that result), I see nothing before us but the exasperation of class animosities, a struggle for pre-eminence, and the ultimate triumph of unrestrained democracy. . . .

Believe me, &c.,

HENRY GOULBURN

Peel *Memoirs*, ii.201-4

4   The Background to Peel's Decision

Peel's detailed proposal, in a fourth memorandum of 2 December, for a gradual progressive reduction in the duties on grain until they were finally extinguished, won over all his colleagues except Lord Stanley and the Duke of Buccleuch. Since Peel considered that the unanimous support of the cabinet was indispensable for the success of his policy, he resigned office on 5 December. Russell hesitantly accepted a commission to form a government but encountered difficulties both of personalities and policy. He abandoned his task and Peel resumed office on 20 December. The memorandum written by Prince Albert five days later refers to a long conversation the previous day when, elated by his success in retaining all his old cabinet except Stanley, the prime minister had obviously spoken with great freedom. Though some allowance should be made for Albert's tendency to interpret casual conversation in rather absolute terms, there is no reason to suspect the basic reliability of his account. Peel's opinions had shifted considerably between 1842 and 1845 and it was probably an accepted view among his close confidants (Graham, Lord Lincoln, Sidney Herbert) that the next step in corn policy would be total repeal. Lincoln in fact proposed to Peel on 5 November the course which Albert says Peel had been considering before the potato disease precipitated events.

It is to his *own* talent and firmness that Sir Robert will owe his success, which cannot fail. He said he had been determined not to go to a general election with the fetters the last election had imposed upon him, and he had meant at the end of the next Session to call the whole Conservative Party together and to declare this to them, that he would not meet another Parliament pledged to the maintenance of the Corn Laws, which could be maintained no longer, and that he would make a public declaration to this effect before another general election came on. This had been defeated by events coming too suddenly upon him, and he had no alternative but to deal with the Corn Laws before a national calamity would *force* it on. The League had made immense progress, and had enormous means at their disposal. If he had resigned in November, Lord Stanley and the Protectionists would have been prepared to form a Government, and a Revolution might have been the consequence of it. Now they felt that it was too late.

Sir Robert has *an immense scheme in view*; he thinks he shall be able to remove the contest entirely from the dangerous ground upon which it has got – that of a war between the manufacturers, the hungry and the poor against the landed proprietors, the aristocracy, which can only end in the ruin of the latter; he will not bring forward a measure upon the Corn Laws, but a much more comprehensive one. He will deal with the whole commercial system of the country. He will adopt the principle of the League, *that of removing all protection and abolishing all monopoly* but not in favour of one class and as a triumph over another, but to the benefit of the nation, farmers as well as manufacturers. He would begin with cotton, and take in all the necessaries of life and corn amongst them. The experiments he had made in 1842 and 1845 with boldness but with caution had borne out the correctness of the principle: the wool duty was taken off, and wool sold higher then ever before; foreign cattle were let in, and the cattle of England stood better in the market than ever. He would not ask for compensation to the land, but wherever he could give it, and at the same time promote the social development, there he would do it, but on that ground.

Memorandum by Prince Albert, Windsor Castle, 25 Dec. 1845 in *Letters of Queen Victoria*, ed. A. C. Benson and Viscount Esher (1908), ii.65–6

5. Peel's Explanation in the House of Commons

The speech from which these extracts are taken was given in the debate on the third reading of the Corn Importation bill which was marked by one of Disraeli's most brilliant and merciless pieces of invective and savage interruptions of the prime minister's speech which almost broke his self-control. It was the last of six great speeches (on 22 and 27 January, 16 February, 27 March, 4 May and 15 May) with which Peel sustained his policy through the preliminary discussions, the committee stage, and the second and third readings. After the January speeches, in which his specific corn proposals were merely items in a general complex programme of tariff reform and agricultural compensation, Peel was faced with the defection of two-thirds of his party and a bitter parliamentary contest in which the debates continually centred on the personal issues of political consistency and party leadership. His last four speeches were noticeably sharper and more uncompromising. The series of extracts below summarise his final attitude on the need and justification of repeal.

My belief, therefore, is, that in seeking the re-enactment of the existing law after its suspension, you would have had to contend with greater difficulties than you anticipate. Still I am told, 'You would have had a majority.' I think a majority might have been obtained. I think you could have continued this law, notwithstanding these increased difficulties, for a short time longer; but I believe that the interval of its maintenance would have been but short, and that there would have been, during the period of its continuance, a desperate conflict between different classes of society; that your arguments in favour of it would have been weak; that you might have had no alternative at an early period, had the cycle of unfavourable harvests returned – and who can give an assurance that they would not? – that you might at an early period have had no alternative but to concede an alteration of this law under circumstances infinitely less favourable than the present to a final settlement of the question. . . . It was the foresight of these consequences – it was the belief that you were about to enter into a bitter and, ultimately, an unsuccessful struggle, that has induced me to think that for the benefit of all classes, for the benefit of the agricultural class itself, it was desirable to come to a permanent and equitable settlement of this question. These are the motives on which I acted. I know the penalty to which I must be subject for having so acted; but I declare, even after the continuance of these debates, that I am only the more impressed with the conviction that the policy we advise is correct. . . . Sir, I do not rest my support of this bill merely upon the temporary ground of scarcity in Ireland. I do not rest my support of the bill upon that temporary scarcity, but I believe that scarcity left no alternative to us but to undertake the consideration of this question; and that consideration being necessary, I think that a permanent adjustment of the question is not only imperative, but the best policy for all concerned. . . . Now, all of you admit that the real question at issue is the improvement of the social and moral condition of the masses of the population; we wish to elevate in the gradation of society that great class which gains its support by manual labour – that is agreed on all hands. The mere interests of the landlords – the mere interests of the occupying tenants, important as they are, are subordinate to the great question – what is calculated to increase the comforts, to improve the condition, and elevate the social character of the millions who subsist by manual labour, whether they are engaged in manufactures or in agriculture? . . . My earnest wish has been, during my tenure of power, to impress the people of this country with a belief that the legislature was animated by a sincere desire to frame its legislation upon the principles of equity and justice. I have a strong belief that the greatest object which we or any other government can contemplate should be to elevate the social condition of that class of the people with whom we are brought into no direct relationship by the exercise of the elective franchise. I wish to convince them that our object has been so to apportion taxation, that we shall relieve industry and labour from any undue burden, and transfer it, so far as is consistent with the public good, to those who are better enabled to bear it.

Peel *Speeches*, iv.689-96 (15 May 1846)

6 A Famous Peroration

On 25 June, a few hours after the corn bill passed the House of Lords, the government was defeated on the Protection of Life (Ireland) bill. Peel had already made it plain to his colleagues (memorandum of 21 June) that the government no longer had the power to carry on normal administration and that he was opposed to the policy of dissolving parliament and fighting a general election on the issues of either Irish coercion or free trade. He resigned on 27 June and on Monday 29th announced this to the House of Commons in a speech the concluding passage of which is given here. He had earlier made a deliberate reference to Cobden as the man whose name should be associated with the success of repeal: a tribute which gave great offence, as did to a lesser extent the closing sentences of the speech. 'His unnecessary panegyric of Cobden, his allusion to the selfish monopolists, and his clap-trap about cheap bread in the peroration, exasperated to the last degree his former friends and adherents, were unpalatable to those he had kept, were condemned by all parties indiscriminately', wrote Greville. This was a general upper-class view: it was not shared by the public at large. In the next half-dozen years the peroration was reproduced endlessly until it became the most quoted passage of all Peel's speeches.

In relinquishing power, I shall leave a name, severely censured I fear by many who, on public grounds, deeply regret the severance of party-ties - deeply regret that severance, not from interested or personal motives, but from the firm conviction that fidelity to party engagements - the existence and maintenance of a great party constitutes a powerful instrument of government: I shall surrender power severely censured also, by others who, from no interested motive, adhere to the principle of protection, considering the maintenance of it to be essential to the welfare and interests of the country: I shall leave a name execrated by every monopolist who, from less honourable motives, clamours for protection because it conduces to his individual benefit; but it may be that I shall leave a name sometimes remembered with expressions of good will in the abodes of those whose lot it is to labour, and to earn their daily bread by the sweat of their brow, when they shall recruit their exhausted strength with abundant and untaxed food, the sweeter because it is no longer leavened by a sense of injustice.

Peel *Speeches*, iv.716-17

VIII

INDUSTRY AND SOCIAL PROBLEMS

1 Children in Mines and Collieries

In 1840 Lord Ashley secured the appointment by the Whig government of a Commission to enquire into the employment of children in mines and manufactures. The first report, dealing with mines and collieries, was issued in May 1842. Ashley's speech was delivered on 7 June when moving for leave to bring in a bill to regulate the employment of women and children in mines and was largely based on the evidence printed by the commissioners. Conditions in the mines varied greatly from district to district, as did the attitude of the mine-owners – from the wealthy aristocratic owners of the north-east with a patriarchal interest in their men to the small pit-owners of Yorkshire, Lancashire and Staffordshire often working on insufficient capital and divorced from the men by the system of contracting with gangs, each under their foreman or 'butty'. It was here that some of the most degraded and brutal conditions were encountered. Women and girls were not employed underground in the great coalfields of Northumberland and Durham, nor in Leicestershire, Derbyshire and other areas of the midlands and south-west. The largest proportion of women and girls and some of the most animal forms of work were in Scotland. The conditions depicted below therefore were the worst, not the universal nor possible the most typical conditions. Moreover, most of the women and children came from mining families, and since the miners as a class enjoyed good wages the standard of food and clothing at home was generally (though not always) better than the depiction of conditions underground might suggest.

Sir, the next subject to which I shall request your attention is the nature of the employment in these localities. Now, it appears that the practice prevails to a lamentable extent of making young persons and children of a tender age draw loads by means of the girdle and chain. This practice prevails generally in Shropshire, in Derbyshire, in the West Riding of Yorkshire, in Lancashire, in Cheshire, in the east of Scotland, in North and South Wales, and in South Gloucestershire. The child, it appears, has a girdle bound round its waist, to which is attached a chain, which passes under the legs, and is attached to the cart. The child is obliged to pass on all fours, and the chain passes under what, therefore, in that posture, might be called the hind legs; and thus they have to pass through avenues not so good as a common sewer, quite as wet, and oftentimes more contracted. This kind of labour they have to continue during several hours, in a temperature described as perfectly intolerable. By the testimony of the people themselves it appears that the labour is exceedingly severe; that the girdle blisters their sides and causes great pain. 'Sir,' says an old miner, 'I can only say what the mothers say, it is barbarity – absolute barbarity.' Robert North says, 'I went into the pit at 7 years of age. When I drew by the girdle and chain, the skin was broken and the blood ran down. . . . If we said anything, they would beat us. I have seen many draw at 6. They must do it or be beat. They cannot straighten their backs during the day. I have sometimes pulled till my hips have hurt me so that I have not known what to do with myself.' In the West Riding, it appears, girls are almost universally employed as trappers and hurriers, in common with boys. The girls are of all ages, from 7 to 21. They commonly work quite naked down to the waist, and are dressed – as far as they are dressed at all – in a loose pair of trousers. These are seldom whole on either sex. In many of the collieries the adult colliers, whom these girls serve, work perfectly naked. Near Huddersfield the sub-commissioner examined a female child. He says, 'I could not have believed that I should have found human nature so degraded. Mr Holroyd, and Mr Brook, a surgeon, confessed, that although living within a few miles, they could not have believed that such a system of unchristian cruelty could have existed.' Speaking of one of the girls, he says, 'She stood shivering before me from cold. The rug that hung about her waist was as black as coal, and saturated with water, the drippings of the roof.' 'In a pit near New Mills,' says the sub-commissioner, 'the chain passing high up between the legs of two girls, had worn large holes in their trousers. Any sight more disgustingly indecent or revolting can scarcely be imagined than these girls at work. No brothel can beat it.' – Sir, it would be impossible to enlarge upon all these points; the evidence is most abundant, and the selection very difficult. I will, however, observe that nothing can be more graphic, nothing more touching, than the evidence of many of these poor girls themselves. Insulted, oppressed and even corrupted, they exhibit, not unfrequently, a simplicity and a kindness that render tenfold more heart-rending the folly and cruelty of that system that has forced away these young persons, destined, in God's providence, to holier and happier duties, to occupations so unsuited, so harsh, and so degrading. . . .

Surely it is evident that to remove, or even to mitigate, these sad evils, will require the vigorous and immediate interposition of the legislature. That interposition is demanded by public reason, by public virtue by the public honour, by the public character, and, I rejoice to add, by the public sympathy: for never, I believe, since the first disclosure of the horrors of the African slave-trade, has there existed so universal a feeling on any one subject in this country, as that which now pervades the length and breadth of the land in abhorrence and disgust of this monstrous oppression. It is demanded, moreover, I am happy to say, by many well-intentioned and honest proprietors – men who are anxious to see those ameliorations introduced which, owing to long-established prejudices, they have themselves been unable to effect. From letters and private communications which I have received on the subject, I know that they will hail with the greatest joy such a bill as I shall presently ask leave to introduce.

> Lord Ashley in the House of Commons,
> 7 June 1842, from *Speeches of the Earl of
> Shaftesbury* (1868), pp. 36-45

2   Public Reaction to Disclosure of Conditions in the Coal Mines

The first report of the commissioners became one of the most famous Blue Books of the century (P. P. 1842 XV-XVII). Under the shock of its revelations, aided by Ashley's powerful and affecting speech in the House of Commons on 7 June, the press and public at large (including the Queen and Prince Albert, who sent Ashley a private message of encouragement) gave their support for immediate remedial legislation. This extract from the Tory *Quarterly Review* gives a characteristic press reaction. The bill introduced by Ashley passed both Houses by the first week of August. It encountered opposition from the powerful and well-organised coal interest of the north-east and Ashley's original proposals were modified in detail, partly by compromises in the Commons and partly by amendments in the Lords. Nevertheless the act was a landmark in the field of industrial legislation. Unlike earlier factory laws which regulated hours and conditions of work, the Mines and Collieries Act of 1842 took the absolute course of banning women and girls altogether from underground work, and boys up to the age of ten. Other regulating and safety measures were inserted in the act, including the power to appoint mines inspectors who were to make regular reports to the Secretary of State. Although only one appointment was initially made, that of H. S. Tremenheere, it was an important one since Tremenheere, a former assistant poor law commissioner was a senior and influential official. His reports and recommendation, aided by public reaction to colliery accidents and periodic agitation in parliament, led finally to the foundation in 1850 of a proper corps of coalmines inspectors.

Here, by three ponderous folios, we have disclosed to us – in our own land, and within our own ken – modes of existence, thoughts, feelings, actions, sufferings, virtues, and vices, which are as strange and as new as the wildest dreams of fiction. The earth seems now for the first time to have heaved from its entrails another race, to astonish and to move us to reflection and to sympathy.

Here we find tens of thousands of our countrymen living apart from the rest of the world – intermarrying – having habits, manners, and almost a language, peculiar to themselves – the circumstances surrounding their existence stamping and moulding mind and body with gigantic power. The common accidents of daily life are literally multiplied to this race of men a hundredfold; while they are subject to others which have no parallel on earth. It is not, then, a matter for wonder that their minds should borrow from the rocks and caverns they inhabit something of the hardness of the one and something of the awful 'power of darkness' of the other; and that their hearts and emotions should exhibit the fierceness of the elementx amidst which they dwell.

It is mainly to Lord Ashley, who has headed this great movement for the moral improvement of the working classes, that we are indebted for these volumes, issued apparently for the purpose of letting the public know the true condition of the mining population, and so forcing, by the weight of opinion and individual co-operation, society at large to attempt an amelioration.

The legislature of past years has undoubtedly been to blame in taking no cognizance of such a state of things as is now exhibited. But are they blameless who employ these men, and reap the benefit of labours which have induced a premature old age in their service? Have they, with so much in their power, fulfilled their duties – have they considered how to strengthen the connection of the master and the hireling by other ties than those of gain? Has our Church, clerical and lay, been diligent in civilising these rough natures? Have proprietors, enriched by the development of minerals enabled the Church to increase her functionaries in proportion to the growth of new populations? These are questions which must be asked, and answered, before the burden of change is laid on a few, which should be borne by many. We feel that this benefit must be conferred by all; and the power of the state must be propped by the self-denial of the owner – and the mild, untiring energies of the Church must be aided by the kindly influences of neighbourhood – before it can be hoped that such a race as the miners can be brought to abandon their rooted prejudices and brutal indulgences. Living in the midst of dangers – and on that account supplied with higher wages, and with much leisure to spend them – they unite in their characters all that could flow from sources which render man at once reckless and self-indulgent – a hideous combination, when unleavened by religion and the daily influences of society – little likely to be removed by Acts of Parliament alone, and never if Acts of Parliament find none but official hands to aid in enforcing them. . . .

If there was anything which could tinge with a deeper hue these scenes and deeds, it would be the possibility that all such evils might be inflicted on women; and so they are in the following districts, which we purposely name: – 1. West Riding of York, southern part; 2. Bradford and Leeds; 3. Halifax; 4. Lancashire; 5. South Wales; 6. East of Scotland.

In the last of these provinces the whole state of the mines as to care, ventilation, draining, and as to employment of women, reads so miserably that we fain would hope the account overdrawn.

[A number of examples of the conditions in which women and girls worked in the pits, similar to those given by Lord Ashley, were quoted from the Report.]

But we will not multiply these spectacles of human misery and degradation; and to whom can they be traced? Is the contractor alone in fault? –is the proprietor scatheless? Or shall we blame the parents and relations, by whose avarice and improvidence, according to Mr Sub-commissioner Scriven (p. 74, App. I), in almost every instance, these females are thus subjected to moral and physical evils of the worst kind? On both sides the guilt is great – very great – but surely vastly greater in him who has not even the excuse of poverty for receiving 'the thirty pieces of silver'. The example of discontinuing this hateful practice has, however, been set in what we must consider as the very worst district. No sooner did the abomination come to the knowledge of the Duke of Buccleuch than his grace commanded its utter abolition in all his collieries; and the same course was immediately followed by the family of Dundas of Arniston, and others of his neighbours: –

'Until the last eight months,' says William Hunter, overman in a colliery at Arniston, 'women and lassies were wrought below in these works, when Mr Alexander Moxton, our manager, issued an order to exclude them from going below, having some months prior given intimation of the same. Women always did the lifting, or heavy part of the work, and neither they nor the children were treated like human beings; nor are they where they are employed. Females submit to work in places where no man nor even lad could be got to labour in: they work in bad roads up to their knees in water, in a posture nearly double: they are below till the last hour of pregnancy: they have swelled ankles and haunches, and are prematurely brought to the grave, or, what is worse, a lingering existence. Many of the daughters of miners are now at respectable service. I have two who are in families at Leith, and who are much delighted with the change.' – Ibid. p. 94.

No wonder! And we trust many more proprietors will now be encouraged to follow such examples, especially as it can be proved to the able-bodied husband and father that there is no necessity for him to lose anything at all by a change so beneficial to his wife and children.

The Duke of Buccleuch's manager, Mr James Wright, says: –

'I feel confident that the exclusion of females will advantage the collier in a physical point of view, and that it will force the alteration of the economy of the mines. Owners will be compelled to alter their system. They will ventilate better, make better roads, and so change the system as to enable men who now work only three or four days a-week to discover their own interest in regularly employing themselves. *Since young children and females have been excluded from his Grace's mines, we have never had occasion to increase the price of coal.'*

> Quarterly Review, lxx (1842), 158 seq. (article on Report of the Commissioners for Enquiry into the condition of Children employed in Mines etc.)

3   The Campaign for the Ten Hours Bill

Since 1830 there had been strong agitation especially in Yorkshire for the limitation of the work first of children and later of women to ten hours. Led initially by humanitarians like Wood, Oastler, Bull and Sadler, it was linked through the machinery of regional Short Time Committees to the Trades Unions who sought immediately the creation of more work for the men and ultimately the practical limitation of all factory hours. In 1833 was passed the first major factory act, which forbade the employment of children under nine, restricted the hours of young persons (13-18) to twelve *per diem* (69 per week) and set up a system of factory inspection. The operation of the act was the object of much controversy and factory reformers led in parliament by Lord Ashley pressed for further restrictions. After the failure of Graham's factory bill in 1843 as a result of the educational dispute, the government introduced a new bill in February 1844. Children's work was limited to 6½ hours per diem to allow time for schooling; women were brought under the same protective restrictions as young persons (including the limitation to twelve hours); and among other safety measures, employers were compelled to fence dangerous machinery. In committee Lord Ashley carried a clause against the government reducing the legal maximum for young persons to ten hours. The government brought in an almost identical bill, making it an issue of confidence. When Ashley again moved a ten hours amendment on the third reading of the bill on 10 May he was defeated by 297-159 and the bill passed.

HOUSE OF COMMONS
May 10, 1844

On moving 'That the Clause (And be it Enacted, That from and after the 1st day of October in the present year, no young person shall be employed in any Factory more than eleven hours in any one day, or more than sixty-four hours in any one week; and that from and after the 1st day of October, 1847, no young person shall be employed in any Factory more than ten hours in any one day, or more than fifty-eight hours in any one week; and that any person who shall be convicted of employing a young person for any longer time than is in and by this Clause permitted, shall for every such offence be adjudged to pay a penalty of not less than £-, and not more than £-,) be now read a second time.'

It may seem to be almost superfluous, after three distinct declarations of this House (and in a single session), to appeal again, by rhetoric or argument to your feelings or understanding. We determined only seven weeks ago, three times, actually, that the period of labour should be less than twelve hours; and twice, virtually, that it should not exceed ten. The world at large believed that a middle term would be offered; but her Majesty's Ministers have refused concession – they have invited, nay, more, have compelled us to revive the debate, and now summon the House of Commons to revoke its decision. . . .

Sir, I cannot but be aware that enough has been said on the physical and social condition of the people – one way or the other, the minds of all are fully made up; and it is, indeed, unnecessary to say more, as all, even the hottest of my opponents, admit that a reduction of the hours of labour, could it be effected without injury to the workmen and manufacturers, would be highly desirable. The only objection, then, in the

minds of many honourable and thinking men, is the danger to the
people themselves; and I find myself in the condition of being summoned to refute the charge that I, who propose the scheme, am far more
inhuman than those who resist it. . . .

Now, after all that has been written and said on the subject, I can
discover no more than four arguments urged by our opponents
against this measure – all of which are comprised in the Manchester
Petition lately presented to this House.

1st. That the passing of a ten hours' bill would cause a diminution of
produce.

2nd. That there would take place a reduction, in the same proportion,
of the value of the fixed capital employed in the trade.

3rd. That a diminution of wages would ensue, to the great injury of
the workmen.

4th. A rise of price, and consequent peril of foreign competition.

Even supposing that these assertions be separately, they cannot be
collectively, true; it is very fair to place before us a variety of possible
contingencies, but it must not be urged that we are threatened by a
combination of them. Any one event may occur; but such an occurrence
prevents, in one case at least, the full accomplishment of the other. . . .

Now, Sir, I have long been regarded as a monomaniac on these
subjects, as a man of peculiar opinions, one having a fixed idea, but
without support, or even countenance, in my wild opinions – yet is it
not the fact that the reduction of the hours of labour is a question
maintained and desired by many great manufacturers in the cotton
trade? I may quote in this House the members for Oldham, Salford,
Ashton, and Blackburn – I will just indicate a few without its walls,
firm friends of the measure; Mr Kay, of Bury; Mr William Walker, of
Bury, perhaps the largest consumer of cotton in that district; Mr
Hamer, of the same place, a partner in the firm of the late Sir Robert
Peel; Mr Cooper, of Preston; Mr Tysoe, of Salford; and Mr Kenworthy,
of Blackburn. I set great store by the opinions of this gentleman last
named, because he has passed through all the gradations of the business,
and has by his own talent and integrity raised himself from the condition of an operative to the station of a master. I may add, too, the
name of Mr Hargreaves, of Accrington – no inconsiderable person in
Lancashire – who feels so strongly on this subject, that he attended a
public meeting in support of the question, and moved a resolution
himself.

Speeches of the Earl of Shaftesbury (1868), pp•
116–27

4 Industrial Conditions in Manchester: An Independent Witness

C. C. F. Greville (1794-1865) is one of the great political diarists in British history. He was an intelligent, independent-minded aristocrat, belonging to a younger branch of the family of the Earls of Warwick. Educated at Eton and Christ Church, Oxford, he began his career as private secretary to Earl Bathurts and from 1821 to 1859 was Clerk to the Privy Council, where his work brought him into contact with all the leading politicians of the day. He also was a well-known race-horse owner and a minor literary figure. His *Journals of the Reigns of George IV, William IV and Queen Victoria*, collectively known as the *Greville Memoirs*, published with some omissions by Henry Reeve between 1875 and 1887 and re-edited in full by L. Strachey and R. Fulford in seven volumes in 1938, comprise the best contemporary political commentary of the period. At the time of writing the following, he was guest at Worsley, in south Lancashire the house of Lord Francis Egerton, the heir to the great industrial fortunes of the 3rd Duke of Bridgwater who had developed the coal-mines and built subterranean canals in that area.

(Nov. 1845)

I have passed these few days in seeing this place and some of the manufacturing wonders at Manchester. . . . On Wednesday I went through the subterraneous canal, about a mile and a half long, into the coal-pit, saw the working in the mine, and came up by the shaft; a black and dirty expedition, scarcely worth the trouble, but which I am glad to have made. The colliers seem a very coarse set, but they are not hard worked and, in fact, do no more than they choose. There are many miles of this underground canal. On Thursday I went to Manchester, and saw one of the great cotton and one of the great silk manufactories; very curious even to me, who am ignorant of mechanics, and could only stare and wonder, without being able to understand the niceties of the beautiful and complicated machinery by which all the operations of these trades are performed. The heat of the rooms in the former of them was intense, but the man who showed them to us told us it was caused by the prodigious friction and the room might be much cooler, but the people liked the heat. Yesterday I went to the infant school, admirably managed; then to the recreation-ground of the colliers and working-hands – a recent establishment. It is a large piece of ground, planted and leveled round about what is called the paying house, where the men are paid their wages once a fortnight. The object is to encourage sports and occupations in the open air, and induce them not to go to the ale-house. There are cricket, quoits, and football, and ginger-beer and coffee are sold to the people, but no beer or spirits.

This has only a partial success. Afterward to Patricroft, to see Messrs Nasmyth's great establishment for making locomotive engines, every part of which I went over. I asked at all the places about the wages and habits of the workpeople. In Birley's cotton factory 1,200 are employed, the majority girls, who earn from ten to fourteen shillings a week. At Nasmyth's the men make from twenty to thirty-two shillings a week. They love to change about, and seldom stay very long at one place; some will go away in a week, and some after a day. In the hot factory rooms the women look very wan, very dirty, and one should guess very miserable. They work eleven hours generally, but though it might be thought that domestic service must be preferable, there is the greatest difficulty in procuring women-servants here. All the girls go to the factory in spite of the confinement, labor, close atmosphere, dirt, and moral danger which await them. The parents make them go, because they earn money which they bring home, and they like the independence and the hours every evening, and the days from Saturday to Monday, of which they can dispose.

Greville Memoirs, 22 November 1845

5   The Ten Hours Act and its Supporters

Despite the setback in 1844 Lord Ashley introduced a Ten Hours bill in January 1846 which was eventually defeated after he had resigned his seat on the issue of the Corn Laws. After the fall of Peel's administration Fielden took charge of a new bill in 1847 which passed with large majorities through both houses (9 and 10 Vic. cap. 29). From May 1848 the daily hours of work for women and young persons in mills and factories were restricted to ten (58 in the week). Although a feature of the campaign from the start had been the support of local Conservatives and Anglicans, the movement had drawn on a wide cross-section of society. Oastler was a Tory Anglican, Sadler a Tory Wesleyan, Bull an Anglican parson, Fielden a Liberal Quaker. Among the manufacturers who lent their aid, Hindley and Brotherton were Liberal M.P.s, Wood a Tory Anglican. In the House of Lords a large number of bishops attended the debate on the second reading of the bill to give it support. 'This will do very much to win the hearts of the manufacturing people to Bishops and Lords,' wrote Ashley in his diary; 'it has already converted the hard mind of a Chartist Delegate'. Subsequent evasion of the act by the use of 'relays' of operatives to keep mills at work throughout the legally permitted limits of the working day (5.30 a.m. to 8.30 p.m.) led in 1849–50 to a renewal of agitation and several judicial test-cases. The issue was settled by a government act of 1850 imposing stricter limits of the working day (6 a.m. to 6 p.m.) with 1½ hours for meals but in return allowing a 10½ hour working day with a maximum of 60 hours per week.

At a General Meeting of the Lancashire Central Short Time Committee, held at the house of Mr Thomas Wilkinson, Red Lion Inn, Manchester, on Tuesday evening, 8 June 1847, the following resolutions were unanimously adopted.

1. That this Committee feel deeply thankful to the disposer of all good gifts, for the glorious success which has attended their efforts to ameliorate the condition of the women and children employed in factories, and sincerely congratulate their fellow-labourers in the good work on the peaceful and constitutional character of the agitation, as well as the triumphant manner in which the Ten Hours' Bill has passed the British Parliament.

2. That the hearty thanks of this Committee are due, and are hereby gratefully tendered on behalf of the working people of Lancashire, to the Right Honourable Lord Ashley, for his zealous and efficient services in this sacred cause, during a period of fourteen years of constant, consistent, and exemplary perseverance, to improve the moral, religious, and mental condition of the factory workers by endeavouring to obtain for them leisure hours to be devoted to that purpose; and especially for the zeal and activity he has displayed during the present session of Parliament.

3. That the best thanks of this Committee are also due to John Fielden, Esq., M.P., for the honest, consistent and straightforward conduct which he has ever pursued on behalf of his poorer fellow-countrymen; and especially for his exertions during the present session of Parliament in bringing the agitation for the Ten Hours' Bill to a successful issue.

4. That this Committee tender their heartfelt thanks to the Right Honourable the Earl of Ellesmere and Lord Faversham, for their zealous exertions in conducting the Ten Hours' Bill safely through the House of Lords.

5. That this Committee are deeply grateful and tender their best thanks to J. Brotherton, Esq., M.P., H. A. Aglionby, Esq., M.P., C. Hindley, Esq., M.P., and all those members who spoke and voted in favour of this measure during its progress in the House of Commons.

6. That this Committee are deeply impressed with the gratitude they owe to the Duke of Richmond, the Bishops of Oxford, London, and St. Davids, and all the peers who spoke and voted in favour of the Ten Hours' Bill.

7. That this Committee offer their most hearty congratulations and sincere thanks to John Wood, Richard Oastler, W. Walker, Thomas Fielden, and Joseph Gregory, Esqrs., and to the Rev. G. S. Bull, for their support of this cause in times when it was unpopular to be ranked amongst its advocates; and also to all its friends and supporters out of Parliament.

8. That this Committee view with extreme satisfaction the past support of the clergy of the Established Church, as well as of those ministers of religion of all denominations who were ever found amongst the supporters of this measure, and sincerely hope that they will live to see realised the happy results which we believe were the aim and object of all their pious labours in this cause. . . .

PAUL HARGREAVES, Chairman

[From *The Ten Hours' Advocate*, 12 June 1847]

J. C. Gill, *The Ten Hours Parson* (1959), Appendix B. Reprinted by courtesy of S.P.C.K.

IX

URBANISATION AND ADMINISTRATIVE REFORM

1   The Metropolitan Police Act, 1829

In 1822 Peel as Home Secretary secured a select committee to enquire into the state of the police and the increase of crime in the metropolis. Its report (July 1828) for the first time officially recommended a radical reform and extension of the police. The main recommendations were the creation of a central police office under two magistrates freed from all other duties; the amalgamation of all the regular police forces in the London area (excluding the City); and the defrayment of the cost of the new establishment partly from parochial rates, and partly from the Treasury. A bill founded on the report became law in June 1829. An ex-officer, Colonel Charles Rowan, and a young barrister, Richard Mayne, became the first Commissioners as the two new police magistrates were styled; and plans were set on foot for a force of over one thousand men. The new metropolitan police were uniformed but armed only with truncheons. Despite the obstructionism of some parochial authorities and the hostility of the London mob, they soon won the approval of influential public opinion; and a parliamentary committee set up to enquire into the Cold Bath Fields riots of 1833 reported strongly in their favour. The metropolitan police headquarters in Whitehall Place had a back-entry in Scotland Yard generally used by the police which soon gave the popular name to the whole building.

An Act for improving the Police in and near the Metropolis
[19 June 1829]

Whereas Offences against Property have of late increased in and near the Metropolis; and the local Establishments of Nightly Watch and Nightly Police have been found inadequate to the Prevention and Detection of Crime, by reason of the frequent Unfitness of the Individuals employed, the Insufficiency of their Number, the limited Sphere of their Authority, and their Want of Connection and Co-operation with each other: And whereas it is expedient to substitute a new and more efficient System of Police in lieu of such Establishments of Nightly Watch and Nightly Police, within the Limits herein-after mentioned, and to constitute an Office of Police, which, acting under the immediate Authority of One of His Majesty's Principal Secretaries of State, shall direct and control the whole of such new System of Police within those Limits: Be it therefore enacted. . . . That it shall be lawful for His Majesty to cause a new Police Office to be established in the City of *Westminster*, and by Warrant under His Sign Manual to appoint Two fit Persons as Justices of the Peace of the Counties of *Middlesex, Surrey, Hertford, Essex,* and *Kent,* and of all Liberties therein, to execute the Duties of a Justice of the Peace at the said Office, and in all Parts of those several Counties, and the Liberties therein, together with such other Duties as shall be herein-after specified, or as shall be from Time to Time directed by One of His Majesty's Principal Secretaries of State, for the more efficient Administration of the Police within the Limits herein-after mentioned. . . .

IV. . . . the whole of the City and Liberties of *Westminster*, and such of the Parishes, Townships, Precincts, and Places in the Counties of *Middlesex, Surrey,* and *Kent,* as are enumerated in the Schedule to this Act, shall be constituted, for the Purposes of this Act, into One District, to be called 'The Metropolitan Police District'; and a sufficient Number of fit and able Men shall from Time to Time, by the Directions of One of His Majesty's Principal Secretaries of State, be appointed as a Police Force for the whole of such District. . . .

V. . . . the said Justices may from Time to Time, subject to the Approbation of One of His Majesty's Principal Secretaries of State, frame such Orders and Regulations as they shall deem expedient, relative to the general Government of the Men to be appointed Members of the Police Force under this Act. . . .

XXIII, XXX. [Magistrates appointed under the act to have powers to levy a rate not exceeding 8d. in the pound on rateable value in all places of which the new police have taken charge.]

Statutes, 10 Geo. IV cap. 44

2 The New Poor Law, 1834

The Poor Law Amendment Act of 1834 was the classic example of the fundamental Whig-Benthamite reforming legislation of the period. Preceded by the massive and well-publicised report of a Royal Commission it received general parliamentary support and passed into law with comparatively little discussion. The machinery of the new law in itself constituted a virtual administrative revolution: a central commission not under direct ministerial or parliamentary control, with wide powers to establish efficient local administrative units, supervise the work of locally elected guardians, prescribe the qualifications of local officials, and make regulations for the general administration of relief. The principles on which the commissioners were to act are not defined in the act but followed from the recommendations of the earlier report: the principle of 'less eligibility' (i.e. that workhouse conditions should be made less preferable than those of the lowest paid labourer), the prohibition of outdoor relief (i.e. relief outside the workhouse), the segregation of different classes of paupers (including the separation of married couples), and the abolition of the 'rate-in-aid' (i.e. grants to supplement low wages).

For political and administrative reasons it proved impossible to apply these principles rigorously, particularly in the northern and midland industrial districts. As early as 1837 the commissioners modified their instructions to permit outdoor relief at Nottingham, where the creation of the new poor-law union coincided with a period of acute unemployment; and in 1841 a general order was issued to a number of northern unions prescribing rules for the administration of outdoor relief to able-bodied men, half of which was to be in kind (bread, potatoes etc.), in return for some form of supervised work. In practice the local boards of guardians in both town and country enjoyed a greater latitude in the administration of relief than commonly supposed. The widespread belief that assistance could only be obtained by entering the workhouse (the workhouse test) was completely erroneous. In 1841, of the 1,300,000 persons who received relief, only 192,000 were in workhouses, the remaining 1,108,000 being assisted in their own homes. Of the total sum of £3,884,000 spent in poor relief from the rates, only £892,000 was expended in the workhouses, while nearly £3 millions were spent in outdoor relief. The figures for 1839 and 1840 show similar proportions.

An Act for the Amendment and better Administration
of the Laws relating to the Poor in *England* and *Wales*
[14 August 1834]

It shall be lawful for His Majesty, His Heirs and Successors, by Warrant under the Royal Sign Manual, to appoint Three fit Persons to be Commissioners to carry this Act into execution. . . .

II. . . . the said Commissioners shall be styled 'The Poor Law Commissioners for *England* and *Wales*'; and the said Commissioners, or any Two of them, may sit, from Time to Time as they deem expedient, as a Board of Commissioners for carrying this Act into execution. . . .

V. ... the said Commissioners shall once in every Year, submit to One of the Principal Secretaries of State a general Report of their Proceedings; and every such general Report shall be laid-before both Houses of Parliament. ...

XV. ... from and after the passing of this Act the Administration of Relief to the Poor throughout *England and Wales*, according to the existing Laws, or such Laws as shall be in force at the Time being, shall be subject to the Direction and Control of the said Commissioners; and for executing the Powers given to them by this Act the said Commissioners shall and are hereby authorized and required, from Time to Time as they shall see Occasion, to make and issue all such Rules, Orders, and Regulations for the Management of the Poor, for the Government of Workhouses and the Education of the Children therein, and for the Management of Parish Poor Children. ...

XVI. ... no General Rule of the said Commissioners shall operate or take effect until the Expiration of Forty Days after the same, or a Copy thereof, shall have been sent, signed and sealed by the said Commissioners, to One of His Majesty's Principal Secretaries of State; and if ... His Majesty, with the Advice of His Privy Council, shall disallow the same or any Part thereof, such General Rule, or the Part thereof so disallowed, shall not come into operation. ...

XXIII. ... it shall be lawful for the said Commissioners ... by and with the Consent in Writing of a Majority of the Guardians of any Union, or with the Consent of a Majority of the Rate-payers and Owners of Property ... to order and direct the Overseers or Guardians of any Parish or Union not having a Workhouse or Workhouses to build a Workhouse or Workhouses ...

XXVI. .·. it shall be lawful for the said Commissioners, by Order under their Hands and Seal, to declare so many Parishes as they may think fit to be united for the Administration of the Laws for the Relief of the Poor, and such Parishes shall thereupon be deemed a Union for such Purpose, and thereupon the Workhouse or Workhouses of such Parishes shall be for their common Use. ...

XXXVIII. ... where any Parishes shall be united by Order or with the Concurrence of the said Commissioners ... a Board of Guardians of the Poor for such Union shall be constituted and chosen, and the Workhouse or Workhouses of such Union shall be governed, and the Relief of the Poor in such Union shall be administered, by such Board of Guardians; and the said Guardians shall be elected by the Rate-payers, and by such Owners of Property in the Parishes forming such Union as shall in manner herein-after mentioned require to have their Names entered as entitled to vote as Owners in the Books of such Parishes respectively; and the said Commissioners shall determine the Number and prescribe the Duties of the Guardians to be elected in each Union, and also fix a Qualification without which no Person shall be eligible as such Guardian. . . .

XXXIX. . . . if the said Commissioners shall, by any Order under their Hands and Seal, direct that the Administration of the Laws for the Relief of the Poor of any single Parish should be governed and administered by a Board of Guardians, then such Board shall be elected and constituted, and authorized and entitled to act, for such single Parish, in like Manner. . . .

XLII. . . . the said Commissioners may and are hereby authorized, by Writing under their Hands and Seal, to make Rules, Orders, and Regulations, to be observed and enforced at every Workhouse already established. . . .

XLVI. . . . it shall be lawful for the said Commissioners . . . to direct the Overseers or Guardians of any Parish or Union . . . to appoint such paid Officers with such Qualifications as the said Commissioners shall think necessary for superintending or assisting in the Administration of the Relief and Employment of the Poor. . . .

XLVII. . . . the said Commissioners may . . . as and when they shall think proper, by Order under their Hands and Seal, either upon or without any Suggestion or Complaint in that Behalf from the Overseers or Guardians of any Parish or Union, . . . remove any Master of any Workhouse, or Assistant Overseer, or other paid Officer of any Parish or Union whom they shall deem unfit . . . or incompetent. . . .

LII. And whereas a Practice has obtained of giving Relief to Persons or their Families who, at the Time of applying for or receiving such Relief, were wholly or partially in the Employment of Individuals, and the Relief of the able-bodied and their Families is in many Places administered in Modes productive of Evil in other respects: And whereas Difficulty may arise in case any immediate and universal Remedy is attempted to be applied in the Matters aforesaid; be it further enacted, That from and after the passing of this Act it shall be lawful for the said Commissioners, by such Rules, Orders, or Regulations as they may think fit, to declare to what Extent and for what Period the Relief to be given to able-bodied Persons or to their Families in any particular Parish or Union may be administered out of the Workhouse of such Parish or Union, by Payments in Money, or with Food or Clothing in Kind, or partly in Kind and partly in Money, and in what Proportions, to what Persons or Class of Persons, at what

Times and Places, on what Conditions, and in what Manner such Out-door Relief may be afforded. . . .

XCVIII. . . . in case any Person shall wilfully neglect or disobey any of the Rules, Orders, or Regulations of the said Commissioners or Assistant Commissioners, or be guilty of any Contempt of the said Commissioners sitting as a Board, such Person shall, upon Conviction before any Two Justices, forfeit and pay for the First Offence any Sum not exceeding Five Pounds, for the Second Offence any Sum not exceeding Twenty Pounds nor less than Five Pounds, and in the event of such Person being convicted a Third Time, such Third and every subsequent Offence shall be deemed a Misdemeanor, and such Offender shall be liable to be indicted for the same Offence, and shall on Conviction pay such Fine, not being less than Twenty Pounds, and suffer such Imprisonment, with or without hard Labour, as may be awarded against him by the Court by or before which he shall be tried and convicted.

Statutes, 4 & 5 Will. IV cap. 76

3   Reform of Local Government: The Municipal Corporations Act, 1835

The case for a reform of the miscellaneous and often inefficient and oligarchical corporations which governed the towns was overwhelming and never questioned by the responsible leaders of the opposition. But the report of the Commission on Municipal Reform which preceded the drafting of the bill was partisan and in radical eyes the purpose of the act was to complement the effect of the Reform Act of 1832 by securing an actual transfer of power in local politics. Peel and Wellington were more concerned with securing greater efficiency and preventing the towns from falling into the hands of radical demagogues. The proposed municipal electorate of all resident rate-payers was preferred by them to the parliamentary £10 householders but they objected to various other features and a prolonged parliamentary battle took place over details. In the House of Lords the opposition was extremely factious but Peel and Russell combined to achieve a compromise. Some of the amendments accepted by the government – property qualifications for councillors, election of aldermen for six years, nomination of J.P.s by the Crown – probably improved the new corporations as administrative bodies. The act applied only to the 178 existing boroughs but provision was made whereby other towns could come under the act. By 1851, 18 new towns had successfully applied for incorporation, including Birmingham, Bradford, Manchester and Sheffield.

An Act to provide for the Regulation of Municipal
Corporations in *England* and *Wales*

[9 September 1835]

VI. ... after the First Election of Councillors under this Act in any
Borough the Body or reputed Body Corporate named in the said
Schedule in connexion with such Borough shall take and bear the
Name of the Mayor, Aldermen, and Burgesses of such Borough. ...

IX. [All males of full age who had occupied a house, shop, or
warehouse within a borough for two years and were inhabitant
householders in the borough or within seven miles, to qualify for
enrolmen as burgesses on condition of payment of all rates to which
their property was liable.]

XXV.   in every Borough shall be elected, at the Time and in the
Manner herein-after mentioned, One fit Person, who shall be and be
called 'The Mayor' of such Borough; and a certain Number of fit
Persons, who shall be and be called 'Aldermen' of such Borough; and a
certain Number of other fit Persons, who shall be and be called 'The
Councillors of such Borough; and such Mayor, Aldermen, and Councillors for the Time being shall be and be called 'The Council' of such
Borough. . [the council to elect a third of their number as aldermen,
sitting for six years, with provision for the retirement of half the
aldermen every three years.]

XXVII.   Persons in Holy Orders or regular Ministers of Dissenting
Congregations to be ineligible for election to the Council. All councillors and aldermen to be on the burgess roll of the borough and to have
the requisite property qualification, i.e. in the larger boroughs real or
personal estate to the value of £1,000 or rated at an annual value of
£30, in the smaller boroughs £500 or rated at £15.]

XXIX. . . every Burgess of any Borough who shall be enrolled on
the Burgess Roll for the Time being of such Borough shall be entitled
to vote in the Election of Councillors.

XXX. [Burgesses to elect the requisite number of councillors each
year on 1 November, or if a Sunday, 2 November.]

XXXI. [Councillors to sit for three years, a third of their number to
retire each year but to be eligible for re-election.]

XLIX. ... on the Ninth Day of *November* in every year the Council
of the Borough shall elect out of the Aldermen or Councillors of such
Borough a fit Person to be the Mayor of such Borough, who shall
continue in his Office for One whole Year; and in case a Vacancy shall
be occasioned ... by reason of any Person who shall have been elected

to such Office not accepting the same, or by reason of his dying or ceasing to hold the said Office, the Council of the Borough shall within Ten Days after such Vacancy elect out of the Aldermen or Councillors of the said Borough another fit Person to be the Mayor thereof for the Remainder of the then current Year. . . .

LVII. . . . the Mayor for the time being of every Borough shall be a Justice of the Peace of and for such Borough, and shall continue to be such Justice of the Peace during the next succeeding Year after he shall cease to be Mayor, unless disqualified as aforesaid. . . .

LVIII. . . . the Council of every Borough, on the Ninth Day of *November* in this present Year, shall appoint a fit Person, not being a Member of the Council, to be the Town Clerk of such Borough, who shall hold his Office during Pleasure . . . and the Council of every Borough shall in every Year appoint another fit Person, not being a Member of the Council, to be the Treasurer of the Borough, and also such other Officers as have been usually appointed in such Borough, or as they shall think necessary for enabling them to carry into execution the various Powers and Duties vested in them by virtue of this Act. . . .

LXXVI. . . . the Council to be elected for any Borough shall, immediately after their First Election, and . . . thereafter as they shall deem expedient, appoint . . . a sufficient Number of their own Body, who, together with the Mayor of the Borough for the Time being, shall be and be called the Watch Committee for such Borough; . . . and such Watch Committee shall, within Three Weeks after their First Formation, and . . . thereafter as Occasion shall require, appoint a sufficient Number of Fit Men who shall be sworn in before some Justice of the Peace having Jurisdiction within the Borough to act as Constables for preserving the Peace by Day and by Night, and preventing Robberies and other Felonies, and apprehending Offenders against the Peace. . . .

LXXXVI. [The Watch Committee to transmit to the Secretary of State quarterly each year a report of the number, equipment, wages, organisation and regulations of the borough police force.]

LXXXVII. LXXXVIII. [Council to have powers for lighting streets and to raise rates for that purpose.]

XC. . . . it shall be lawful for the Council of any Borough to make such Bye Laws as to them shall seem meet for the good Rule and Government of the Borough, and for Prevention and Suppression of all such Nuisances as are not already punishable in a summary Manner by virtue of any Act in force throughout such Borough, and to appoint by such Bye Laws such Fines as they shall deem necessary for the

Prevention and Suppression of such Offences; provided that no Fine so to be appointed shall exceed the sum of Five Pounds. . . .

XCII. . . in case the Borough Fund shall not be sufficient for the Purposes aforesaid, the Council of the Borough is hereby authorized and required from Time to Time to estimate as correctly as may be, what Amount, in addition to such Fund, will be sufficient for the Payment of the Expenses to be incurred in carrying into effect the Provisions of this Act; and in order to raise the Amount so estimated the said Council is hereby authorized and required from Time to Time to order a Borough Rate in the Nature of a County Rate to be made within their Borough, and for that Purpose the Council of such Borough shall have within their Borough all the Powers which any Justices of the Peace assembled at their General or Quarter Sessions in any County in England have. . . .

XCIX. . . . if the Council of any Borough shall think it requisite that a salaried Police Magistrate or Magistrates be appointed within such Borough, such Council is hereby empowered to make a Bye Law fixing the Amount of the Salary which he or they are to receive in that Behalf. . . .

Statutes, 5 & 6 Will. IV cap. 76

4   Urban Conditions: An Epoch-making Report, 1842

The attention of poor law authorities in London was early drawn to the effect of disease and insanitary conditions in producing destitution. Following a local survey based on London, reports of which were laid before the Home Secretary, Bishop Blomfield of London (who had been chairman of the Commission of Enquiry into the Poor Law) moved in the House of Lords (August 1839) for a national enquiry. The Report of 1842 which resulted was prepared by Chadwick on the basis of voluminous material supplied by poor law officials and medical practitioners in different parts of the country. A Health of Towns bill based on its findings was introduced by the government in 1845 but eventually lapsed with the fall of Peel's ministry the following year. A similar bill introduced by the Whigs in 1847 was also withdrawn, though smaller piece-meal legislation was passed in 1846-8. The main legislative consequence was the Public Health Act of 1848, facilitating the erection of local Boards of Health with statutory powers and setting up a central Board of Health composed of Lord Morpeth, an able and sympathetic Whig minister, Chadwick, and Lord Ashley. The central Board could do little more than exhort, advise and assist local efforts and met with considerable obstruction. The mishandling of the cholera epidemic in London in 1849 further weakened Chadwick's position. In 1854 the Board was subordinated to the Privy Council and in 1858 abolished, its functions being divided between the Privy Council and the Home Office. Though hampered, the work of the Board had not been negligible. By the end of 1853 the number of towns which had petitioned to come under the act was 284, of which 182 had already qualified.

(a)   SANITATION (pp. 46-7)

The first question I generally put when a new case of fever is admitted, is as to the locality. I was struck with the number of admissions from Market-street; most of the cases coming from that locality became quickly typhoid, and made slow recoveries. This is a narrow back street; it is almost overhung by a steep hill, rising immediately behind it; it contains the lowest description of houses, built closely together, the access to the dwellings being through filthy closes. The front entrance is generally the only outlet. Numerous food for the production of miasma lies concealed in this street. I think I could point out one in each close.

In one part of the street there is a dunghill, – yet it is too large to be called a dunghill. I do not misstate its size when I say it contains a hundred cubic yards of impure filth, collected from all parts of the town. It is never removed; it is the stock-in-trade of a person who deals in dung; he retails it by cartfuls. To please his customers, he always keeps a nucleus, as the older the filth is the higher is the price. The proprietor has an extensive privy attached to the concern. This collection is fronting the public street; it is enclosed in front by a wall; the height of the wall is about 12 feet, and the dung overtops it; the malarious moisture oozes through the wall, and runs over the pavement. The effluvia all round about this place in summer is horrible. There is a land of houses adjoining, four stories in height, and in the summer each house swarms with myriads of flies; every article of food and drink must be covered, otherwise, if left exposed for a minute, the flies immediately attack it, and it is rendered unfit for use, from the strong taste of the dunghill left by the flies.

Evidence of Dr Laurie on Greenock.

(b)   LIVING CONDITIONS (pp. 124-5)

Mr Riddall Wood was examined as to the effects of over-crowded tenements on the moral habits observed in the course of his visits from house to house in the various towns he was engaged to examine: –

'In what towns did you find instances of the greatest crowding of the habitations? – In Manchester, Liverpool, Ashton-under-Lyne, and Pendleton. In a cellar in Pendleton, I recollect there were three beds in the two apartments of which the habitation consisted, but having no door between them, in one of which a man and his wife slept; in another, a man, his wife and child; and in a third two unmarried females. In Hull I have met with cases somewhat similar. A mother about 50 years of age, and her son I should think 25, at all events above 21, sleeping in the same bed, and a lodger in the same room. I have two or three instances in Hull in which a mother was sleeping with her grown up son, and in most cases there were other persons sleeping in the same room, in another bed. In a cellar in Liverpool, I found a mother and her grown-up daughters sleeping on a bed of chaff on the ground in one corner of the cellar, and in the other corner three sailors had their bed. I have met with upwards of 40 persons sleeping in the same room, married and single, including, of course, children and several young adult persons of either sex. In Manchester I could enumerate a variety of instances in which I found such promiscuous mixture of the sexes in sleeping-rooms.'

(c)   OCCUPATIONAL MORTALITY (pp. 200-1)

The difference in the proportions of ages between a depressed and unhealthy and a comparatively long-lived and strong population, is shown in the following comparative view of the ages of the miners and of the 1043 non-mining labourers who were living and working: –

	30 Years of Age and under 40	40 Years and under 45	45 Years and under 50	50 Years and under 55	55 Years and under 60	60 Years and under 70	70 Years and under 80	80 Years and up-wards
Miners 1652	772	377	239	125	56	29	1	
Labourers 1043	695	422	Not given	284	Not given	144	48	7
	Per cent	Per cent	Per cent	Per cent	Per cent	Per cent	Per cent	Per cent
Miners	47	23	14	$7\frac{1}{2}$	$3\frac{1}{2}$	$1\frac{1}{2}$		
Labourers	67	41		27		14	$4\frac{1}{2}$	$\frac{1}{2}$

So that whilst in every 100 men of the younger population of work-people there would not be 2 men of the experience beyond sixty years of age, not 8 above fifty, or not a fourth passed forty; in the older population there would be 14 beyond sixty, 27 beyond fifty, or a clear majority of mature age, and, it may be presumed, of the comparatively staid habits given by age. Dr Scott Allison found that the average age of the living male heads of families of the *collier* population at Tranent whose condition he has contrasted with that of the agricultural population, and whose ages he could ascertain, was 34 years; whilst the average age of the living male heads of the agricultural families was 51 years and 10 months. He considers that the like proportions would be found to be more extensively prevalent, and would serve as fair indications of the relative condition of the different populations.

Whenever the adult population of a physically depressed district, such as Manchester, is brought out on any public occasion, the preponderance of youth in the crowd and the small proportion of aged, or even of the middle aged, amongst them is apt to strike those who have seen assemblages of the working population of other districts more favourably situated.

In the course of some enquiries under the Constabulary Force Commission as to the proportions of a paid force that would apparently be requisite for the protection of the peace in the manufacturing districts, reference was made to the meetings held by torchlight in the neighbourhood of Manchester. It was reported to us, on close observation by peace-officers, that the bulk of the assemblages consisted of mere boys, and that there were scarcely any men of mature age to be seen amongst them. . . . But on ascertaining the numbers qualified for service as special constables, the gloomy fact became apparent, that the proportion of men of strength and of mature age for such service were but as a small group against a large crowd, and that for any social influence they were equally weak. The disappearance by premature deaths of the heads of families and the older workmen at such ages as those recorded in the returns of dependent widowhood and orphanage, must to some extent practically involve the necessity of supplying the lapse of staid influence amidst a young population by one description or other of precautionary force.

(d)   AN ENLIGHTENED EMPLOYER (p. 255)

Mr Samuel Greg, at Bollington, has formed baths for the use of his workpeople, which he thus describes:

'The bathing-room is a small building, close behind the mill, about 25 feet by 15. The baths, to the number of seven, are ranged along the walls, and a screen about six feet high, with benches on each side of it, is fixed down the middle of the room. The cold water is supplied from a cistern above the engine-house, and the hot water from a large tub which receives the waste steam from the dressing-room and is kept constantly at boiling temperature. A pipe from each of these cisterns opens into every bath, so that they are ready for instant use. The men and women bathe on alternate days; and a bath-keeper for each attends for an hour and a half in the evening. This person has the entire care of the room, and is answerable for everything that goes on in it. When any one wishes to bathe he comes to the counting-house for a ticket, for which he pays a penny, and without which he cannot be admitted to the bathing-room. Some families, however, subscribe a shilling a-month, which entitles them to five baths weekly; and these hold a general subscriber's ticket, which always give him admittance to the room. I think the number of baths taken weekly varies from about 25 to 70 or 80.'

(e)   CONCLUSIONS AND REMEDIES (pp. 369-72)

I beg leave to recapitulate the chief conclusions which that evidence appears to me to establish.

First, as to the extent and operation of the evils which are the subject of the inquiry: –

That the various forms of epidemic, endemic, and other disease caused, or aggravated, or propagated chiefly amongst the labouring classes by atmospheric impurities produced by decomposing animal and vegetable substances, by damp and filth, and close and overcrowded dwellings prevail amongst the population in every part of the kingdom, whether dwelling in separate houses, in rural villages, in small towns, in the larger towns – as they have been found to prevail in the lowest districts of the metropolis. . . .

That high prosperity in respect to employment and wages, and various and abundant food, have afforded to the labouring classes no exemptions from attacks of epidemic disease, which have been as frequent and as fatal in periods of commercial and manufacturing prosperity as in any others.

That the formation of all habits of cleanliness is obstructed by defective supplies of water.

That the annual loss of life from filth and bad ventilation are greater than the loss from death or wounds in any wars in which the country has been engaged in modern times. . . .

That the public loss from the premature deaths of the heads of families is greater than can be represented by any enumeration of the pecuniary burdens consequent upon their sickness and death. . . .

That the ravages of epidemics and other diseases do not diminish but tend to increase the pressure of population.

That in the districts where the mortality is the greatest the births are not only sufficient to replace the numbers removed by death, but to add to the population.

That the younger population, bred up under noxious physical agencies, is inferior in physical organization and general health to a population preserved from the presence of such agencies.

That the population so exposed is less susceptible of moral influences, and the effects of education are more transient than with a healthy population.

That these adverse circumstances tend to produce an adult population short lived, improvident, reckless, and intemperate, and with habitual avidity for sensual gratifications.

That these habits lead to the abandonment of all the conveniences and decencies of life, and especially lead to the overcrowding of their homes, which is destructive to the morality as well as the health of large classes of both sexes. . . .

Secondly. As to the means by which the present sanitary condition of the labouring classes may be improved: –

The primary and most important measures, and at the same time the most practicable, and within the recognized province of public administration, are drainage, the removal of all refuse of habitations, streets, and roads; and the improvement of the supplies of water.

That the chief obstacles to the immediate removal of decomposing refuse of towns and habitations have been the expense and annoyance of the hand labour and cartage requisite for the purpose.

That this expense may be reduced to one-twentieth or to one-thirtieth, or rendered inconsiderable, by the use of water and self-acting means of removal by improved and cheaper sewers and drains.

That refuse when thus held in suspension in water may be most cheaply and innoxiously conveyed to any distance out of towns, and also in the best form for productive use, and that the loss and injury by the pollution of natural streams may be avoided.

That for all these purposes, as well as for domestic use, better supplies of water are absolutely necessary. . . .

That the expense of public drainage, of supplies of water laid on in houses, and of means of improved cleansing would be a pecuniary gain, by diminishing the existing charges attendant on sickness and premature mortality.

That for the protection of the labouring classes and of the ratepayers against inefficiency and waste in all new structural arrangements for the protection of the public health, and to ensure public confidence that the expenditure will be beneficial, securities should be taken that all new local public works are devised and conducted by responsible officers qualified by the possession of the science and skill of civil engineers . . .

That for the prevention of the disease occasioned by defective ventilation and other causes of impurity in places of work and other places where large numbers are assembled, and for the general promotion of the means necessary to prevent disease, that it would be good economy to appoint a district medical officer independent of private practice, and with the securities of special qualifications and responsibilities to initiate sanitary measures and reclaim the execution of the law. . . .

That the attainment of these and the other collateral advantages of reducing existing charges and expenditure are within the power of the legislature and are dependent mainly on the securities taken for the application of practical science, skill, and economy in the direction of local public works.

And that the removal of noxious physical circumstances, and the promotion of civic, household, and personal cleanliness, are necessary to the improvement of the moral condition of the population; for that sound morality and refinement in manners and health are not long found co-existent with filthy habits amongst any class of the community.

> Report from the Poor Law Commissioners on an
> Enquiry into the Sanitary Condition of the
> Labouring Population of Great Britain (1842)

5 Town and Country: Taking Stock in 1851

A feature of early-Victorian administrative techniques was the development of statistical science as an instrument not merely for recording crude figures but for eliciting causal connections between social phenomena and providing a more exact basis for social legislation. Apart from the valuable work of various local statistical societies, the main sources of information were (1) the com-

pulsory registration of births, deaths and marriages under the act of 1836 which
also set up a central registry office at Somerset House with a Registrar-General
who presented annual reports to parliament, (2) the census of population held
every decade since 1801. The early and defective censuses were mainly concerned to discover the numbers, locality and sex of the population. In 1831 a
more sophisticated enumeration of occupation was adopted. In 1841 a distinction was made between those born within and without the county of residence.
In the 1851 census, the most detailed and accurate of the series to date, information
was procured not only on occupation but on birthplace, family relationships,
church membership and school-attendance. The 1851 census also formed a
landmark in two other respects. The population of Great Britain had doubled
since the first census of 1801, the fastest rate of growth it was ever to record; and
for the first time the population of the towns equalled that of the countryside.

The most important result which the inquiry establishes, is the addition
in half a century, of *ten millions* of people to the British population.
The increase of population in the half of this century nearly equals the
increase in all preceding ages; and the addition, in the last *ten* years, of
two millions three hundred thousand to the inhabitants of these islands,
exceeds the increase in the last *fifty* years of the eighteenth century.
Contemporaneously with the increase of the population at home,
emigration has proceeded since 1750 to such an extent, as to people
large states in America, and to give permanent possessors and cultivators
to the land of large colonies in all the temperate regions of the world;
where, by a common language, commercial relations, and the multiplied reciprocities of industry, the people of the new nations maintain
an indissoluble union with the parent country. Two other movements
of the population have been going on in the United Kingdom: the
immigration of the population of Ireland into Great Britain, and the
constant flow of the country population into the towns. The current of
the Celtic migration is now diverted from these shores; and chiefly
flows in the direction of the United States of America, where the
wanderers find friends and kindred. The movement of the country
population to the towns, went on unnoticed by the earlier writers, and it
has never yet been clearly exhibited; but it is believed that the Tables
of the birth-place of the inhabitants of the towns and counties, will
determine its extent and character. It is a peculiarity of this movement
in these latter times, that it is directed to new points, where the towns
engage in a manufacture as one vast undertaking, in which nearly the
whole population is concerned; as well as to the County towns, and
to London. . . .

It is one of the obvious physical effects of the increase of population, that the proportion of land to each person diminishes; and the decrease is such that within the last fifty years, the number of acres to *each person* living, has fallen from 5·4 to 2·7 acres in Great Britain; from *four* acres to *two* acres in England and Wales. As a countervailing advantage, the people have been brought into each other's neighbourhood; their average distance from each other has been reduced in the ratio of 3 to 2; labour has been divided; industry has been organized in towns; and the quantity of produce either consisting of, or exchangeable for, the conveniences, elegancies, and necessaries of life has, in the mass, largely increased, and is increasing at a more rapid rate than the population. . . .

At the same time, too, that the populations of the towns and of the country have become so equally balanced in number – *ten millions* against *ten millions* – the union between them has become, by the circumstance which has led to the increase of the towns, more intimate than it was before; for they are now connected together by innumerable relationships, as well as by the associations of trade. It will be seen in the final publication, that a large proportion of the population in the market towns, the county-towns, the manufacturing towns, and the metropolis, was born in the country; and that, in England, town and country are bound together, not only by the intercourse of commerce and the interchange of intelligence, but by a thousand ties of blood and affection.

Census of Great Britian 1851, vol. i (1852),
Report, Section 3 (Some of the General
Results of the Inquiry), lxxxii–lxxxiv

X

A REVOLUTION IN TRANSPORT: THE COMING OF THE RAILWAYS

1 The Advantages of Railways (1832)

The greatest of the early nineteenth-century British technological achievements was the revolution in transport represented by the steam railway. The Stockton-Darlington line (1825) was designed to carry coal from the collieries to coastal transport shipping. The Liverpool-Manchester line (1830), though originally intended mainly for cheap freight transport, was the first regular passenger line. Its financial success was the stimulus to most of the railroads built in the next two decades. Until 1852 over the country as a whole passenger traffic remained more lucrative than freight. The early financing of the Liverpool-Manchester railway is obscure and it is possible that its high dividends (10%) were partly maintained out of borrowed capital. What it did do, however, was to demonstrate the cheapness and safety of the new means of locomotion. The article below, appearing within a couple of years of the opening of the line, was clearly written to convey an encouraging account of what was in effect the first experimental commercial passenger railroad.

Before the establishment of the Liverpool and Manchester railway, there were twenty-two regular and about seven occasional extra coaches between those places, which, in full, could only carry per day 688 persons. The railway, from its commencement, carried 700,000 persons in eighteen months being an average of 1,070 per day. It has not been stopped for a single day. There has occurred but one fatal accident on it in eighteen months. The fare by coach was 10s. inside, and 5s. outside – by railway it is 5s. inside, and 3s. 6d. outside. The time occupied in making the journey by coach was four hours – by railway it is one hour and three quarters. All the coaches but one have ceased running, and that chiefly for the conveyance of parcels. The mails all travel by the railway, at a saving to government of two-thirds of the expense. The railway coaches are more commodious than others. The travelling is cheaper, safer, and easier. A great deal of traffic, which used to go by other roads, comes now by railway; both time and money are saved, though the length of the journey may be often increased. The proportion of passengers carried by railway, over those carried by coach, has been as twenty-two to ten, in winter, and seventeen or eighteen to ten in summer. A regiment of soldiers has been carried by the railway from Manchester to Liverpool in two hours. Gentlemen's carriages are conveyed on trucks by the railway. The locomotives travel in safety after dark. The rate of carriage of goods is 10s. per ton; by canal it used to be 15s. per ton. The time occupied in the journey by railway is two hours; by canal it is twenty hours. The canals have reduced their rates 30 per cent. Goods delivered in Manchester the same day they are received in Liverpool. By canal they were never delivered before the third day. By railway, goods, such as wines and spirits are not subject to the pilferage which existed on the canals. The saving to manufacturers in the neighbourhood of Manchester, in the carriage of cotton alone, has been 20,000l. per annum. Some houses of business save 500l. a year in carriage. Persons now go from Manchester to Liverpool and back in the same day with great ease. Formerly they were generally obliged to be absent the greater part of two days. More persons now travel on their own business. The railway is assessed to the parochial rates in all the parishes through which it passes; though only thirty-one miles, it pays between 3,000l. and 4,000l. per annum in parochial rates. Coal pits have been sunk, and manufactories established on the line, giving great employment to the poor; manufactories are also erected on the line, giving increased employment, and thus reducing the number of claimants for parochial relief. The railway pays one-fifth of the poor-rates in the parishes through which it passes; fresh coal-mines sunk, owing to facilities of carriage, and price reduced. It is found advantageous for the carriage of milk and garden produce; arrangements about to be made for milk to be carried fifteen miles at 1s. for ten gallons, (i.e. less than one farthing per quart). A great deal of land on the line has been let for garden ground, at increased rents. Residents on the line find the railway a great convenience, by enabling them to attend to their business in Manchester and Liverpool with ease, at little expense. No inconvenience is felt by residents from smoke or noise; and, on the contrary, great advantage is experienced by means of travelling, to and fro, distances of ten miles in half an hour for 1s. and without any fatigue. The engines only burn coke. The value of land on the line has been considerably enhanced by the operation of the railway; land cannot be purchased but at a large increase in price. It is much sought after for building, &c. The railway company, in their late purchases, have been obliged to pay, frequently, double the

price they originally paid for their land. A great deal of land has been
sold for building, at three times its former value. Much waste land on
the line has been taken into cultivation, and yields a good rent.

Annual Register 1832, Miscellaneous Articles

2   First Impressions of Travelling by Railroad

Between 1835 and 1837 there was something of a railway boom and by the
autumn of 1838 about 500 miles of line were open to the public. The growing
interest of the wealthier classes in the new railway phenomenon is illustrated
by this passage from Greville, one of many contemporary descriptions of first
experiences of travel by rail. Knowsley Park, where he stayed during his visit,
was the seat of Lord Derby, between Liverpool and St. Helens. The line he
travelled on from Birmingham was the recently opened Grand Junction
Railroad to Warrington, where a line connected with the Liverpool-Manchester
railway at Newton Junction. The total distance to Liverpool was 97¼ miles and
the scheduled time for fast trains 4½ hours with six intermediate stops.

Knowsley, Tired of doing nothing in London, and of hearing about the
Queen, and the elections, I resolved to vary the scene and run down
here to see the Birmingham railroad, Liverpool, and Liverpool races.
So I started at five o'clock on Sunday evening, got to Birmingham at
half-past five on Monday morning, and got upon the railroad at half-
past seven. Nothing can be more comfortable than the vehicle in
which I was put, a sort of chariot with two places, and there is nothing
disagreeable about it but the occasional whiffs of stinking air which it is
impossible to exclude altogether. The first sensation is a slight degree of
nervousness and a feeling of being run away with, but a sense of security
soon supervenes, and the velocity is delightful. Town after town, one
park and *château* after another are left behind with the rapid variety of a
moving panorama, and the continual bustle and animation of the
changes and stoppages make the journey very entertaining. The train
was very long, and heads were continually popping out of several
carriages, attracted by well-known voices, and then came the greetings
and exclamations of surprise, the 'Where are you going?' and 'How on
earth came you here?' Considering the novelty of its establishment,
there is very little embarrassment, and it certainly renders all other
travelling irksome and tedious by comparison. It was peculiarly gay at
this time, because there was so much going on. There were all sorts of
people going to Liverpool races, barristers to the assizes, and candidates
to their several elections. . . .

I remained at Knowsley till Saturday morning, when I went to Liverpool, got into the train at half-past eleven, and at five minutes after four arrived at Birmingham with an exact punctuality which is rendered easy by the great reserved power of acceleration, the pace at which we travelled being moderate and not above one half the speed at which they do occasionally go; one engineer went at the rate of forty-five miles an hour, but the Company turned him off for doing so.

Greville Memoirs, 18 & 25 July 1837

3   An Early Railway Timetable

George Bradshaw, the originator of railway timetables, was an engraver and printer at Manchester. The first Bradshaw's *Railway Time Tables and Assistant to Railway Travelling* was published on 19 October 1839. The table reproduced here is from the second issue of the third time-table dated 25 October 1839. It contained route maps, town plans, coach fares in London, Liverpool and Birmingham, and a table to enable passengers to reckon their speed in m.p.h. by timing the train over a quarter of a mile in seconds. The railroads for which full timetables were given were the London and Birmingham, the Grand Junction, Liverpool and Manchester, Great Western, and Newcastle and Carlisle. The London to Birmingham line was started in 1834, opened in instalments from 1837, and completed in September 1838. The London terminus was at Euston Grove.

See pp. 168-9

4   A Report of the Railway Department (1842)

Between 1844 and 1847 there was another burst of railway construction and by 1848 about 5,000 miles of line were in operation in the United Kingdom, of which about 400 were in Ireland. The dangers both of wasteful competition and of monopoly were beginning to be appreciated and the advisability of state control seriously debated. Parliamentary acts were necessary to authorize construction and normally prescribed maximum charges but there was virtually no general legislation or control. Following a select parliamentary committee in 1839 acts were passed in 1840 and 1842, placing the existing legal powers of the state in the hands of a railway department of the Board of Trade. These powers were primarily designed to protect the interests of the travelling public. The department had the right of inspection, collected statistics of traffic and accidents, and could initiate legal proceedings for neglect or illegality. But it had no jurisdiction of its own and though it inspected new projects, parliament continued to retain its own control through its private bills committees. A

Distance from Birmingham.	BIRMINGHAM TO LONDON. STATIONS.	**Mixed Short. 6 20 a.m.*		*Mixed Class. 6 a.m.*		**Mail. 8½ a.m.*		*Mixed, calling at 1st class S. 10 a.m.*		*Mixed Class. 12 p.m.*	
Miles		H.	M.	H.	M.	H.	M.	H.	M.	H.	M.
	BIRMINGHAM	..		6	0	8	30	10	0	12	0
12¼	HAMPTON	..		6	25	..		..		12	25
18¼	COVENTRY	..		6	50	9	17	10	45	12	50
23¼	BRANDON	..		7	5	..		..		1	5
29¼	RUGBY	..		7	25	..		11	15	1	25
37	CRICK	..		7	50	..		..		1	50
42¾	WEEDON	..		8	5	10	26	11	55	2	5
49	BLISWORTH	..		8	25	..		12	15	2	25
52½	ROADE	6	20	8	40	..		..		2	40
59¾	WOLVERTON	6	45	9	0	11	11	12	40	3	0
	BLETCHLEY	7	5	9	20	..		..		3	20
71½	LEIGHTON	7	20	9	35	..		1	15	3	35
80½	TRING	7	45	10	0	12	11	1	40	4	0
84½	B. HAMPSTEAD	7	55	10	10	..		..		4	10
87¾	BOXMOOR	8	5	10	20	..		..		4	20
94¾	WATFORD	8	20	10	35	..		2	10	4	35
101	HARROW	8	45	11	0	..		..		5	0
112¼	LONDON	9	30	12	0	1	30	3	30	6	0

There is a *Mixed Train* from Aylesbury to London at 11 *a.m.* and one from London to Aylesbury at 3 *p.m.*

SUNDAY TRAINS.—Times of Departure, Mixed (from Roade) 6 20 a.m, *Mail 8½ a.m, *Mixed 1½ p.m, *Mail, Mix. 12 p.m.

The First Class Trains consist of First Class and Mail Carriages, carrying four inside (one compartment of which is convertible into a Bed Carriage, if required) and of Carriages carrying six inside,—The Mixed Trains consist of First Class Carriages, carrying six inside, and of 2d class carriages *open* at the side, without linings, cushions, or divisions in the compartments.—The Night Mail Train consists of First Class Carriages carrying six inside, and of Second Class Carriages *closed*, and entirely protected from the weather.—Each Carriage has a small roof lamp by day and night.

*Mixed Class. 1¼ p.m.	*First Class. 4 p.m.	Mixed Class. 5 p.m.	First, calling at Mail S. 6 p.m.	*Mail, Mixed. 12 p.m.	FARES.			
					4 in. car. by day, or 1 class 0 in. by night	1st class carriage, 6 inside, by day	2nd class carriage, closed, by night	2nd class carriage, open, by day
H.M.	H.M.	H. M.	H. M.	H. M.	S. D.	S. D.	S. D.	S. D.
1 15	4 0	5 0	6 0	12 0				
1 40	4 25	5 25	6 25	..	3 6	3 0	2 6	2 0
2 0	4 45	5 50	6 45	12 53	5 0	4 6	4 0	3 0
..	..	6 5	..	..	7 0	6 0	5 0	4 0
2 30	5 15	6 25	..	..	8 6	8 0	6 6	5 0
..	..	6 50	..	..	11 0	10 0	8 6	6 6
3 10	5 55	7 5	7 55	2 9	12 6	11 6	9 6	7 6
3 30	3 15	7 25	..	..	14 6	13 0	11 0	8 6
..	..	7 40	..	..	15 6	14 0	11 6	9 6
3 55	3 40	8 0	8 40	2 58	17 6	16 0	13 6	10 6
..	..	8 20	..	..	19 6	17 6	15 0	12 0
..	15	8 35	..	..	21 0	19 0	16 0	12 6
4 55	40	9 0	9 40	4 3	23 6	21 6	18 0	14 6
..	..	9 10	..	..	24 6	22 6	19 0	15 0
..	..	9 20	..	..	25 6	23 6	19 6	15 6
5 25	8 10	9 35	..	..	27 6	25 6	21 0	17 0
..	..	10 0	..	..	29 6	27 0	22 6	18 0
6 45	9 30	11 0	11 30	5 30	32 6	30 0	25 0	20 0

Passengers are especially recommended to have their names and address, or destination, *legibly written* on each part of their Luggage, when it will be placed on the top of the Coach in which they ride, unless it be in a bag, or such other small package as may conveniently be taken under the seats inside, opposite the one they occupy. If the Passenger be destined for Liverpool or Manchester, and has booked his place through, his luggage will be placed on the Liverpool or Manchester coach, and will not be disturbed till it reaches its destination; and to prevent mistakes, the Passenger should shew his ticket to the Porters, and *see* that his luggage is placed on the proper coach.

A passenger having paid his fare, and taken out a ticket, may go by any of the Trains of *that day*, but the ticket will not be available on the following day, unless under special circumstances, when it may be exchanged for a new pass for the day required.

The Trains marked with an asterisk (*) are in conjunction with those of the Grand Junction Railway; sufficient time being allowed at the Birmingham Station, where refreshments are provided, and waiting rooms, with female attendants.

fresh enquiry in 1844 produced a further act which among other provisions authorised the compulsory acquisition of new railways after a period of 21 years. This was to remain a dead letter and the main practical result of the 1844 legislation was the institution of 'parliamentary trains', i.e. the compulsory running of one train in each direction every weekday at a cheap rate of 1d. per mile. For practical purposes the work of the department ceased after 1845 though the Board of Trade retained a general responsibility for railway matters.

(a) Hazards of Railway Travel

Number and Nature of Accidents upon Railways attended with personal injury reported to the Railway Department under the provisions of the Act 3 & 4 Vic. c. 97 for regulating railways.

Class 1 Accidents attended with Personal injury of Danger to the Public arising from causes beyond the control of Passengers.
Total for 1841: 29 Accidents 24 killed 72 injured

Class 2 Accidents attended with Personal injury to Individuals owing to their own negligence or misconduct.
Total for 1841: 36 accidents 17 killed 20 injured

Class 3 Accidents attended with Personal Injury to Servants of the Company under circumstances not involving danger to the Public.

Note: this return is incomplete, as the Board of Trade has not called upon Railway Companies to make returns of accidents which are not of a public nature.
Total for 1841: 60 accidents 28 killed 36 injured.

(summarised report)

From this return, it appears that the number of railway accidents of a public nature has considerably diminished, the last five months of the year 1840 showing 28 accidents, 22 deaths and 131 cases of injury, while the 12 months of 1841 give only 29 accidents, 24 deaths, and 72 cases of injury.... It is very satisfactory to observe, that a marked diminution has taken place in the class of accident, such as collision, arising chiefly from mismanagement or defective arrangements. A great proportion of the accidents which occurred in the end of 1840 and beginning of 1841, were of this nature, no fewer than 17 accidents having occurred in eight months, from August 1840 to April 1841, from the single cause of collisions by trains or engines overtaking others travelling on the same line. During the nine months from April 1841 to January 1842 only five collisions of this nature occurred, and those with one exception unattended with fatal consequence. The diminution in the number of collisions appears too great to be the result of accident, and may fairly be attributed in a considerable degree to the more general adoption of the precautions suggested by the Inspector-General and recommended by this Department, viz. the erection of proper fixed signals at stations, the adoption of a better description of tail-lamps and hand-signals, the enforcement of more attention to signals on the part of servants, and the adoption of proper time tables for all trains including luggage trains, with a view to preserving regularity in the traffic, and proper intervals between successive trains.

The returns of the past year also show a marked diminution in the number of serious accidents occasioned by the misconduct of engine drivers ... This result may be attributed partly to the beneficial result of more extended experience, and of the measures taken by several railway companies, to raise the character of that important class of men, the engine-drivers, and partly to the salutary example of the prosecutions which have been instituted.

P. P. 1842 xli, pp. 15 seq. (*Report of the Officers of the Railway Department to the President of the Board of Trade, February* 1842)

(b) Railways and the Working Classes

In a great majority of cases third-class passengers are conveyed by the same train as other passengers. In fact, the Great Western and London and South Western Railways are the only lines upon which third-class passengers are conveyed exclusively by heavy luggage-trains, and the Directors of the latter Railway have signified their intention of discontinuing the practice immediately and providing accommodation for third-class passengers in the regular passenger trains.

Upon the London and Birmingham Railway, third-class passengers are conveyed by a special train along with cattle, horses, and empty return waggons, but not with heavy luggage trains.

Upon all other lines where third-class passengers are carried, they are taken by mixed trains along with other passengers. ...

With regard to the extent of accommodation afforded to the poorer classes by railways, it will be seen ... that a large third-class traffic is carried on by most of the lines in the manufacturing districts of Yorkshire and Lancashire, in the coal districts of the North, and in Scotland. These lines are in a great measure dependent upon third-class passengers, who are conveyed by all or nearly all the trains at fares averaging from 1d. to $1\frac{1}{4}$d. per mile. ...

The Manchester and Leeds Railway passes through or near 15 towns, between which there were formerly several carts, waggons and vans passing every hour of the day and night, with manufacturing and market produce, of which the humbler people could avail themselves at a trifling expense of money and a considerable sacrifice of time. These are now almost entirely swept away, and the market people load one or more of the railway trucks among them, paying 3d. or 4d. per ton per mile for their goods, and in many instances less than 1d. per mile for themselves. The effect has been to bring a supply of fruit, fish and vegetables within reach of those who could never obtain them formerly, and to afford very great advantages to the market people and towns.

In fine weather respectable tradespeople, clerks, etc., avail themselves of the third-class carriages to a considerable extent; but the bulk of the half a million third-class passengers who are carried on this railway in the course of the year are strictly the working classes, weavers, masons, bricklayers, carpenters, mechanics, and labourers of every description, some of whom used formerly to travel by carts, but the greater number on foot.

The fare from Manchester to London by railway and steam-boat via Hull is 14s; and many of the labouring classes avail themselves of this mode of conveyance, especially during summer. In one respect a remarkable use has been made of the facilities afforded by railway communication. On the occasion of several strikes, when there was a press of work, bodies of workmen have been engaged in London and carried to Manchester, and vice versa. . . .

But upon the long lines, which form the main lines of communication with the metropolis, and upon which there is a great through traffic, the case is very different, and the number of third-class passengers is inconsiderable. The whole number, for instance, of third-class passengers carried on the London and Birmingham and Grand Junction Railways, between London, Manchester and Liverpool, is less than the number carried by the Arbroath and Forfar Railway and not a seventh part of the number carried between Newcastle and North Shields.

Upon these lines it is questionable whether the interests of the proprietors will ever induce them to encourage the development of a large third-class traffic. It is satisfactory, however, to find that there is a growing disposition among railway companies, thus circumstanced, to afford the accommodation of at least one train a day by which the poorer classes may be conveyed at reduced fares. We are informed that the result of the experiment of running a third-class train upon the

London and Birmingham Railway has been very satisfactory, the persons who have availed themselves of it having been, with few exceptions, of a class who could not have afforded to pay second-class fares; and it is expected that the number of this class of passengers will greatly increase when the advantages to be derived from the great saving of time are more generally known.

(*ibid.*, pp. 25 seq.)

5   The Railway Revolution and its Consequences

By 1850 the first great phase of railroad building was over and the main outline of the modern British railway system already in existence. In the preceding year there were 5,500 miles of track open in the United Kingdom. Receipts from passengers amounted to £6 million and from freight (including cattle) £5 million, for the year ending June 1849. In the same year sixty million passengers had been carried, divided into the following categories: First Class 7 million; Second Class 23 million; Third and Parliamentary Class 30 million. A feature of the previous years had been the steady and rapid increase in the number of parliamentary class passengers (i.e. those carried at the compulsory low rate of 1d a mile laid down by statute) from 4 million in 1846 to over 15 million in 1849. Apart from the obvious economic results, and the greater mobility and means of communication afforded to the population at large, the more intangible and pervasive effects on society were beginning to attract the attention of some observers. The author of the following was a conservative-minded barrister whose book *England as It Is* was designed to give a picture of England in its political, social and industrial aspects in the middle of the century as though written for an educated foreigner. He devoted a whole chapter to railways.

(185 1)

The most important event of the last quarter of a century in English history is the establishment of Railroads. The stupendous magnitude of the capital they have absorbed – the changes they have produced in the habits of society – the new aspect they have given, in some respects, to the affairs of government – the new feelings of power they have engendered – the triumphs and the disappointments of which they have been the cause – above all, the new and excessive activities to which they have given rise – must lead all who reflect upon the subject to admit that the importance of the general result of these great under-takings can scarcely be exaggerated. They have done much towards changing the old deliberative and thoughtful habits of Englishmen. People who breakfast at York and dine in London – who may be summoned from Liverpool to the metropolis in three or four minutes

by the electric telegraph, and answer the summons in person within
six or seven hours by the express train – acquire a habit of pressure and
velocity in all they do. . . . Thoughtfulness and prudence are not only
less valued in this country than they were, but they are actually less
valuable so far as regards the attainment of fortune and distinction.
These virtues are *too slow* for the present times. Audacity and quickness
are the qualities in demand. To run risks with cleverness – to dash
through, at all hazards – to do business at all events – to anticipate
profits, and to live as if they were realized – to rush to the point you
would achieve, and there blow off your steam with a prodigious
quantity of noise and vapour – such is now the manner of doing
business in England, and railways have done a great deal towards
establishing this fashion. . . .

. . . The political effects of railways are in many particulars important.
As an investment and absorption of capital they are greatly influential
for good or evil upon the national prosperity. Of late years it has been a
favourite abstract theory of a certain school of politicians, that legislation and government ought to abstain altogether from interference
with the employment of capital, and ought to abolish all laws which
aim at influencing the direction of such employment. It is unquestion-
able that direct interference ought not to be attempted but with great
caution, yet to influence the employment of capital, and to endeavour
to guard the public against employing it foolishly, seems to be a very
important object for a wise government; for how can a nation be
powerful if it be not prosperous, and how can it be prosperous if the
people at large have embarked their capital in foolish undertakings, or
have foolishly embarked capital even in useful undertakings? It appears
to me that, if the legislature had wisely governed the expenditure of
capital upon railways, such a source for the gradual and profitable
investment of profits and savings would have been an immense
national advantage, whereas allowing the public to rush headlong into
undertakings which they had not the means to complete, and for which
the country had no pressing occasion, has been productive of great
private distress, and has no doubt operated most prejudicially upon the
public finances. . . . It seems reasonable to conclude that railroads add
considerably to the power and promptness of executive rule, or at least
they might do so if the government were wielded by men of decision
and vigour. They are instruments by which the power of government
may be brought to bear more quickly, and the results of any stroke of
policy may be more speedily known. In matters of police the advantage
of them has already been experienced in some important cases. They

are productive of such habits of thought and action as render government, in my opinion, more difficult, but they supply, in perhaps yet greater measure, the means of meeting that difficulty. It is required, however, that there should be men capable of using the means.

Whatever has so widely affected the habits of living, and, as I believe, the habits of thought also, of the people, must needs have had an influence on literature; but besides this, the circumstances of railway transit demand a kind of literature of their own, and the supply to meet this demand has been very abundant. . . . Hence arrives the maxim of the publishers, that whoever wants to command an extensive sale for his book must produce something that the railway-traveller can read as he goes along, and use for waste paper at the end of his journey. . . . I believe that to railroads, and to the habits of quick movement in everything, which have grown up in connexion with them, may be fairly attributed much of what is peculiar in the character of our current literature. In particular the light and jesting method of commentary upon public matters – the cloak of caricature with which keen observation so frequently invests itself – arises from the consideration that people are in such a hurry, they must get amusement and criticism at the same time. . . . There are those who think there is nothing more to be admired in the age we live in than the light tone of our practical philosophy, which they regard as a judicious relief from the anxieties of ambition and the pressure of business.

William Johnston, *England As It Is* (1851),
I, 260–76

XI

EPILOGUE

After 1848 there was a noticeable relaxation in the temper of the country. Electoral activity declined with the disruption of the party system; class hostility had decreased; Church and Dissent recognised more clearly the limits of their powers. Cobden and Bright, who had hoped that the national support given to the League could be continued behind a general middle-class programme of reform, found themselves generals without an army and without an effective strategy. Despite the fragmentation of parties, political power remained with the traditional governing classes because they represented the property and influence which could always dominate politics in quiet times. The great psychological pressure generated by the Anti-Corn Law movement had been dissipated in one dramatic crisis; and the passage of repeal helped to reconcile both middle and lower classes to aristocratic parliamentary rule. Peel in the last four years of his life had more national prestige than any minister since the younger Pitt and the accident of his death in 1850 helped to perpetuate the image of the statesman who had sacrificed his career for the country. Even the Duke of Wellington, the object of popular obloquy in 1832, became a venerated national figure. Cobden spoke with some distaste of the 'frenzy of admiration and enthusiasm' with which he was greeted by all classes at the Great Exhibition of 1851. The manufacturers, mollified by the repeal of the corn laws, were learning by experience that factory regulation and inspection were doing them little harm. The Chartist demonstrations of 1848 stimulated into activity by the revolutions on the continent, lacked the stomach for violence and remained without difficulty under police control. What impressed the public was not the menace of the working classes but the solidarity of the middle and upper classes in rallying to the cause of law and order.

For the growing mood of national harmony various explanations were found: the Reform Act of 1832, the repeal of the Corn Laws, the effects of Peel's tariff policy, the Factory Acts, the influence of religion and the activity of the clergy. The problems of the poor had been recognised and a start made in dealing with the grosser evils. Aristocracy and middle class had both shown a sense of social obligations. In the towns reformed municipalities, scientific experts and benevolent employers were in their different ways beginning to make the urban scene more humane and orderly, less obnoxious and lethal. The Great Exhibition of 1851 was made a symbol not only of peace and productivity but also of the unity and interdependence of British society. There was another larger influence at work. The Victorian industrial economy, aided by tariff reforms and the railways, was improving the lot of all classes. After the temporary break caused by the Irish famine the cost of living fell steadily. Even in 1848 it was lower than at any time between Waterloo and 1842. It continued to fall to a point below anything known since 1780. England was not only a pleasanter but a cheaper place to live in than thirty years earlier.

It would be easy to exaggerate. As was to be seen under Gladstone after 1867, the Irish Church was still a vulnerable aspect of the Anglican state church and Dissenters had not yet abandoned the possibility of securing disestablishment and with it real religious equality. Chartism was not entirely dead and the Crimean War saw a recrudescence of middle-class criticism against the aristocratic structure of government. In 1852 there was a long, bitter and unsuccessful strike by the engineers union in London and Lancashire. Nevertheless the worst was over and nineteenth-century England was never again to experience the depths of disunity, violence and distress that marked the first generation after Waterloo. In 1850 the country was on the threshold of the classic High-Victorian period of contentment and prosperity.

1   The Chartist Demonstration in London, 1848

I am sure it is very fortunate that the whole thing has occur'd as it has shewn the good spirit of our middle classes, and almost one may say of the whole population of London, as well as the activity and courage of the aristocracy. 2 hundred Thousand were sworn in special Constables and all higgledy piggledy Peers and Commons, servants, workmen, and all kinds of people, all hale fellow well met an example of union and loyalty and a determination to stand by our constitution which will have a great effect everywhere in England, in Ireland, and in Europe. Besides I think it a positive advantage to bring the higher classes in contact with the lower ones, to see them unite cordially and without pride and ready to stand out in the wet, and the rain, and to fight like Journeymen with no other arms than staffs.

Our Police too are highly gratified to find themselves supported, and to see these specials taking upon themselves as they did the whole police of the Town for 5 hours from 6 to 11 while the real policeman went to their quarters to rest.

Lady Palmerston to Mrs Huskisson, 14 April 1848, in *Letters of Lady Palmerston*, ed. Tresham Lever (1957), John Murray

2   Reflections of a Country Squire on the Year of Revolutions, 1848

11 April (with reference to the Chartist demonstration in London)

Never was so grand and glorious a Demonstration of loyalty of feeling.

All ranks from the Duke to the artificer were associated together in this imposing Band of Special Constables. No French fraternity here. At no period in our history have the upper and middle classes been more united. We may now thank God that the Reform bill has been passed and the Corn Laws repealed. God grant this nation may take warning from the present state of anarchy abroad.

31 December (with reference to the revolutions on the Continent)

Why have we been so wonderfully preserved while Europe has been convulsed to the centre? By the comparative soundness of our social system. The education of the people of this country, tho' sadly defective, is conducted upon *religious principles*. Education abroad is carried on *apart from the Church* and consequently public opinion on the Continent is against government and against religion.

> MS. Diary of W. S. Dugdale of Merevale
> Hall, Warwickshire
> (He was J.P. and deputy lieutenant for his
> county and M.P. for the northern division
> 1832–47.)

3   Snobocracy: Cobden on the Difficulties of Further Radical Advances, 1849

The citadel of privilege in this country is so terribly strong, owing to the concentrated masses of property in the hands of the comparatively few, that we cannot hope to assail it with success unless with the help of the propertied classes in the middle ranks of society, and by raising up a portion of the working-class to become members of a propertied order. . . .

We are a servile, aristocracy-loving, lord-ridden people, who regard the land with as much reverence as we still do the peerage and baronetage. Not only have not nineteen-twentieths of us any share in the soil, but we have not presumed to think that we are worthy to possess a few acres of mother earth. The politicians who would propose to break up the estates of this country into smaller properties, will be looked upon as revolutionary democrats aiming at nothing less than the establishment of a Republic upon the ruin of Queen and Lords. . . .

To me the most discouraging fact in our political state is the condition of the Lancashire Boroughs, where, with the exception of Manchester, nearly all the municipalities are in the hands of the stupidest Tories in

England; and where we can hardly see our way for an equal half-share of Liberal representation in Parliament. We have the labour of Hercules in hand to abate the power of the aristocracy and their allies, the snobs of the towns. I have faith in nothing but slow and heavy toil, and I shall lose all hope if we cannot see with toleration, and a desire to encourage, every effort that aims at curtailing the power and privileges of the common enemy.

Cobden to Bright, October–December 1849, in J. Morley, *Life of Richard Cobden* (1920), pp. 517-22

4 Peel a Proletarian Hero

He fell from official power into the arms of the people, whose enthusiastic plaudits accompanied him, on the evening of his resignation of office, to his residence in Whitehall Gardens. The spontaneous feeling of gratitude and respect which prompted those plaudits has since widened, strengthened, deepened, and will become more and more vivid and intense as the moral grandeur of his motives – the unselfish, self-sacrificing spirit which dictated his public conduct – pierce through, and consume in the clear and brilliant light of that truth and justice which, we are assured by an illustrious authority, has ever inspired his acts, the calumnious misrepresentations so unsparingly heaped upon him. By his humbler countrymen, that testimony to the moral worth of the departed statesman was not waited for, nor needed. They felt instinctively that he must be pure and single minded, as he was intellectually vigorous and great; for what had he, raised aloft upon the bucklers of a powerful and wealthy party, to gain by stooping from that dazzling height, to raise up the humble and lowly from the mire into which ignorant and partial legislation had so long trampled them.

Obituary article on Sir Robert Peel in Chambers' *Papers for the People*, vol. iv, a cheap popular periodical aiming at a mass circulation

5 The Decline of Chartism

Lord Ashley (succ. as 7th Earl of Shaftesbury, 1851) to Lord John Russell

26 November [1851]   Manchester

Chartism is dead in these parts; the Ten Hours Act and cheap provisions have slain it outright. Often as I have seen this people, I never saw them so ardent, so affectionate, so enthusiastic. But then, praised be God, they are *morally* and physically improved. The children look lively and *young*; a few years ago they looked weary and *old*.

Later Correspondence of Lord John Russell, ed.
G. P. Gooch (1925), I, 214

6   The 1851 Exhibition: A National Festival

The Exhibition has been shown to be a great Peace movement, a great moral movement, and a great industrial movement – all of which it most undoubtedly is. Within the last few weeks, a novel and unexpected result has been witnessed, not less gratifying than any other of the more prominent and obvious ones which preceded it.

The classes who could afford to pay for their admission having had their turn, from the holders of season tickets, and the more aristocratic and exclusive visitors who love elbow-room in their amusements, down to the five shilling Saturday people, the half-crown Friday people, and the great bulk of the independent in somewhat humbler circumstances, who congregate on the shilling days, the turn of those who are too poor to pay for such an amusement has come also. Without any infringement of what we must consider the wise and judicious rule of allowing no gratuitous admissions, the doors of the Crystal Palace have been opened to many thousands of industrious, grateful, well-behaved, and admiring people, without cost to themselves. Parties of humble emigrants have come to Hyde Park, in order that they might not take their last look of England without seeing the wondrous Exhibition; and their expenses have been paid by the philanthropic individuals by whose assistance they were enabled to leave the old world for the new. Clergymen and landed proprietors in remote rural districts have organised plans by which whole troops of agricultural labourers, with their wives and children, have been enabled to visit London once in their lives, and to see the marvels of art, skill, and industry congregated together in a building so novel in construction, and so imposing in appearance; and not among the least pleasing of the episodes in the history of the Exhibition has been the appearance of these bucolic or agrarian groups, staring with mute admiration at the splendours of so unusual a spectacle. Manufacturers in the provincial towns, and extensive employers of labour in the metropolis and its environs, have not only given their workpeople a holiday to enable them to visit the

Exhibition, but have in numerous instances paid the expenses both of the trip and of their admission. Wholesale and retail traders have imitated the admirable example. Public companies and schools have done likewise; and bankers, solicitors, and others have remembered the services of their clerks and *employés*, and afforded them both time and the means to partake in the general jubilee. . . . We rejoice to see such examples of kind feeling. They tend to obliterate the jealousies, that, to a greater or less extent, exist between the rich and the poor, and to the fusion of society into one homogeneous and contented mass of mutually related and mutually dependent people. The sympathy manifested by employers for their workpeople throughout the whole country, as well as in the metropolis, has been too general not to have been the spontaneous growth of the national character.

The Illustrated London News, No. 479 (vol. xviii), Saturday, 28 June 1851

Short List of Books for Further Reading

Halévy, E., *History of the English People in the Nineteenth Century*, vols. ii-iv (1926-49)
Young, G. M. (ed.), *Early Victorian England* (2 vols., 1934)

Butler, J. R. M., *The Passing of the Great Reform Bill* (1914)
Gash, N., *Politics in the Age of Peel* (1953)
        Mr Secretary Peel (1961)
        Sir Robert Peel (1972)
        Reaction and Reconstruction in English Politics (1965)
Maccoby, S., *History of Radicalism, 1832-52* (1935)

Brose, O. J., *Church and Parliament* (1959)
Cowherd, R. G., *The Politics of English Dissent* (1956)
Mathieson, W. L., *English Church Reform, 1815-40* (1923)

Briggs, A. (ed.), *Chartist Studies* (1959)
Hovell, M., *The Chartist Movement* (1918)
Mather, F. C., *Public Order in the Age of the Chartists* (1959)

McCord, N., *The Anti-Corn Law League* (1958)
McDowell, R. B., *Public Opinion and Government Policy in Ireland, 1801-46* (1952)
Woodham-Smith, C., *The Great Hunger* (1962)

Driver, C., *Tory-Radical: Life of Richard Oastler* (1946)
Finer, S. E., *The Life and Times of Sir Edwin Chadwick* (1952)
Hammond, J. L. and B., *Lord Shaftesbury* (1923)
Ward, J. T., *The Factory Movement 1830-1855* (1962)

Clapham, J. H., *An Economic History of Modern Britain* vol. 1, *The Early Railway Age, 1820-50* (1926)
Cleveland-Stevens, E., *English Railways* (1915)